HOW TO DRAW
FOR
MINECRAFTERS

CUBE HUNTER

CUBE
HUNTER
WWW.CUBEHUNTER.NET

Rock
Cooper

This Book Belongs to:

Welcome to the start of the journey where you will learn to draw the world of Minecraft! We will start from the simple most easy forms moving towards more complex characters! Here are presented the few tools you will need to accomplish great results... no worries it is nothing special only things that lay around the house! Yay! Can't wait to start!

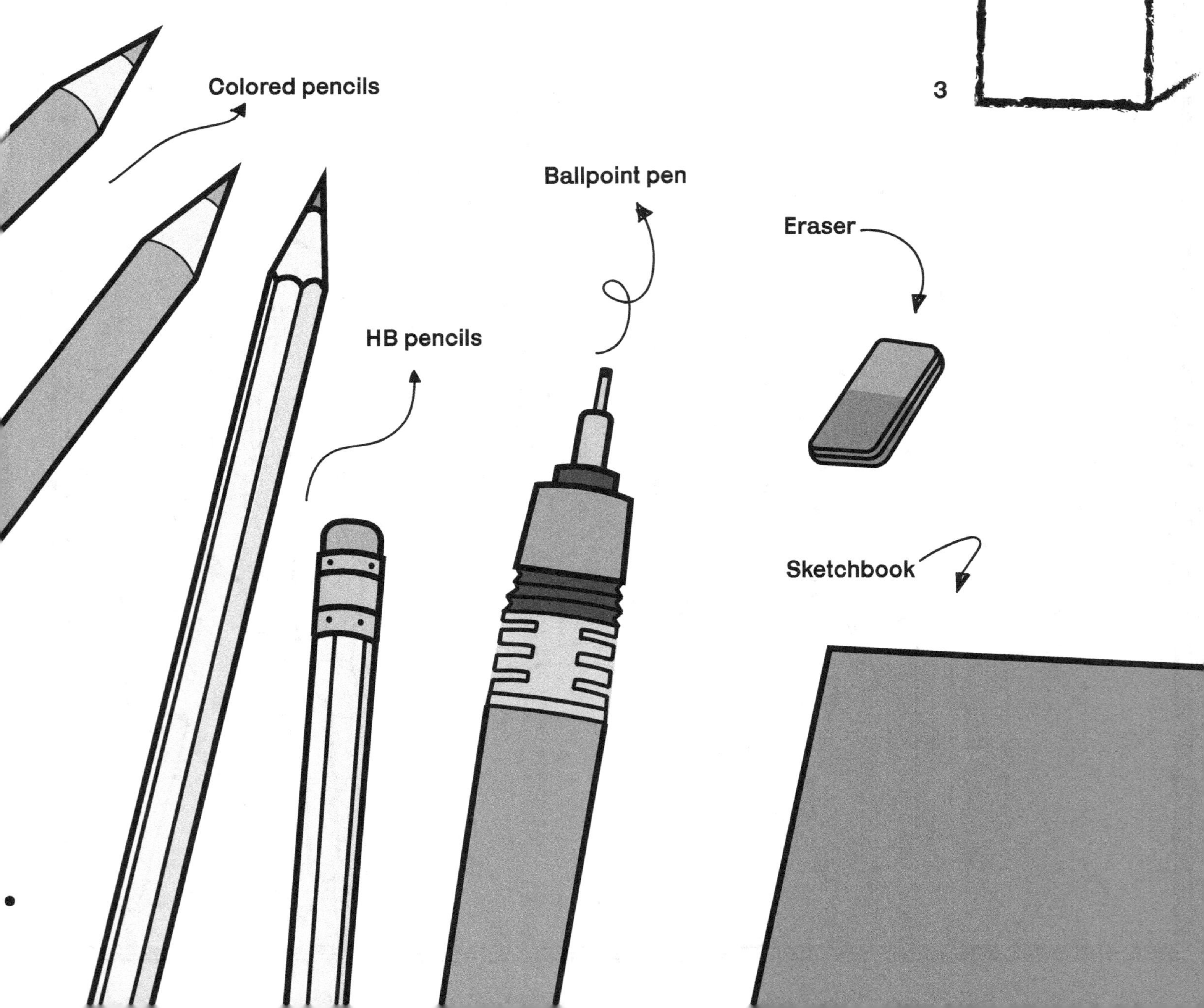

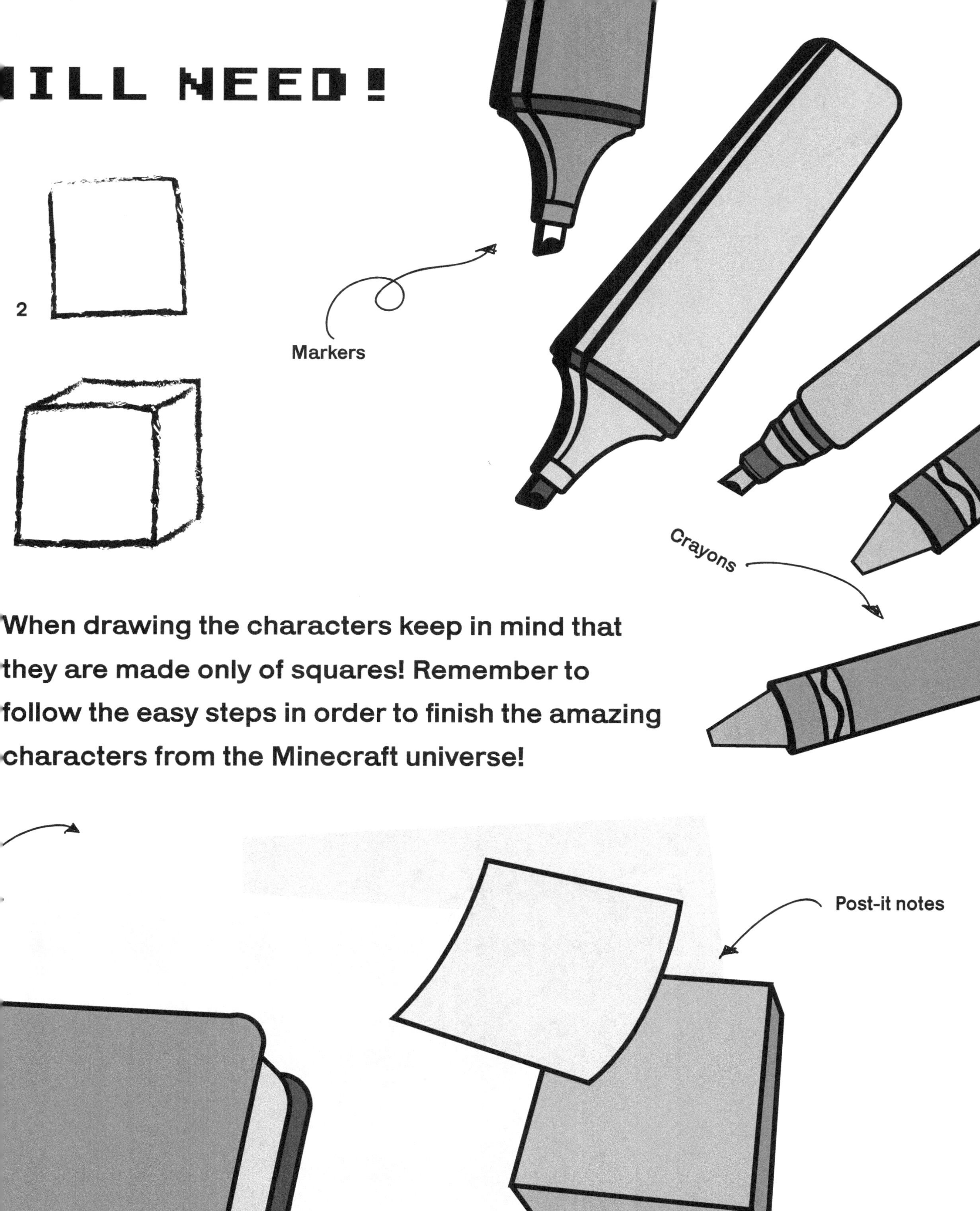

When drawing the characters keep in mind that they are made only of squares! Remember to follow the easy steps in order to finish the amazing characters from the Minecraft universe!

PRACTICE

Following the gray lines to drawing!

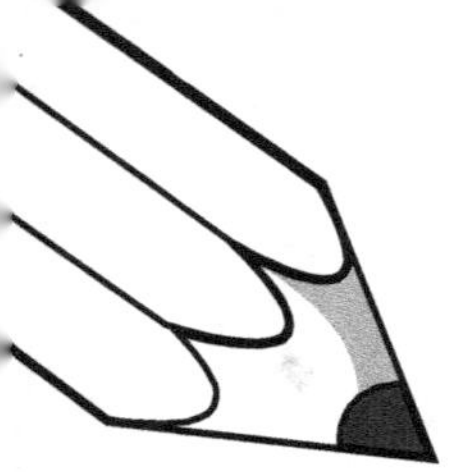

How to draw?
JESSE

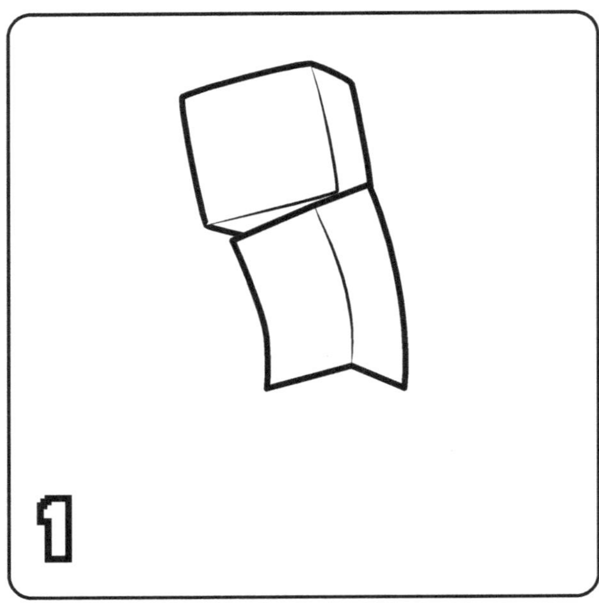

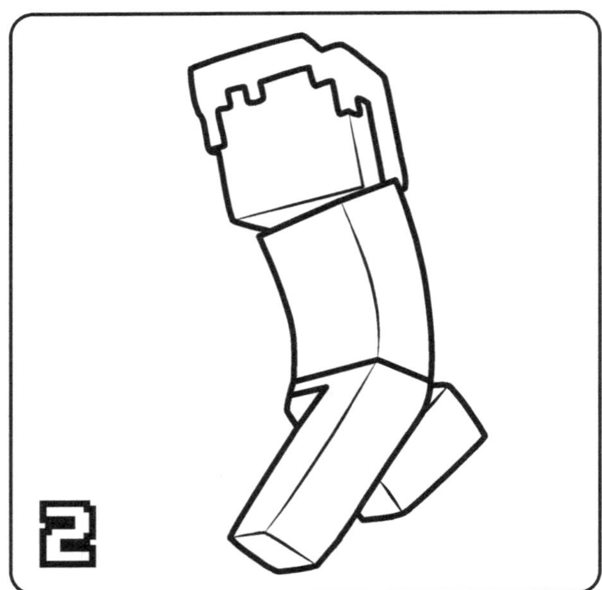

Now, it's your turn

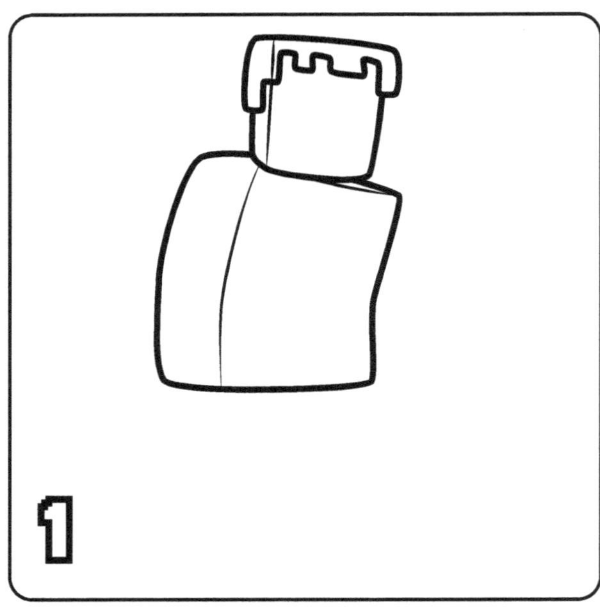

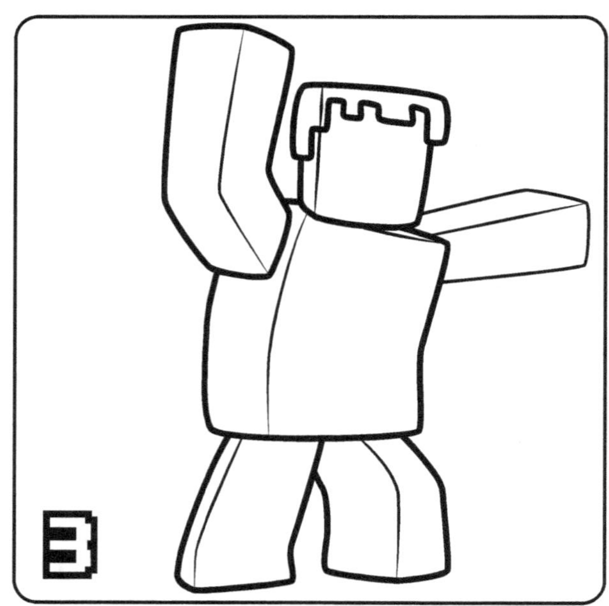

How to draw?
AXEL

Now, it's your turn

How to draw?
BIG HENRY

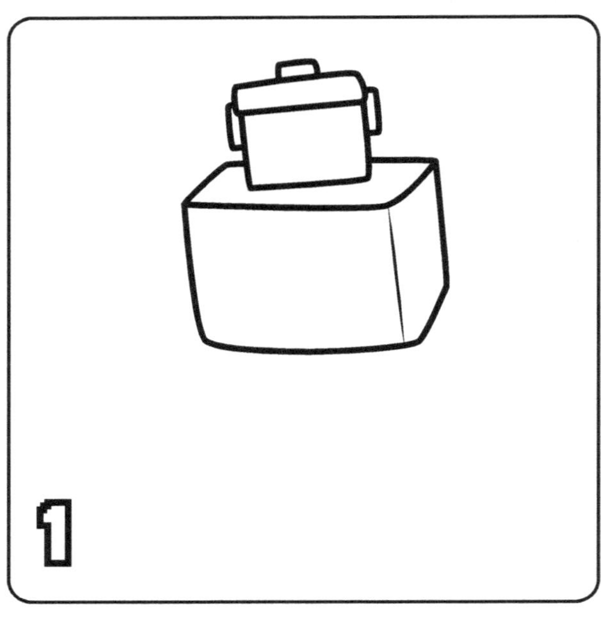

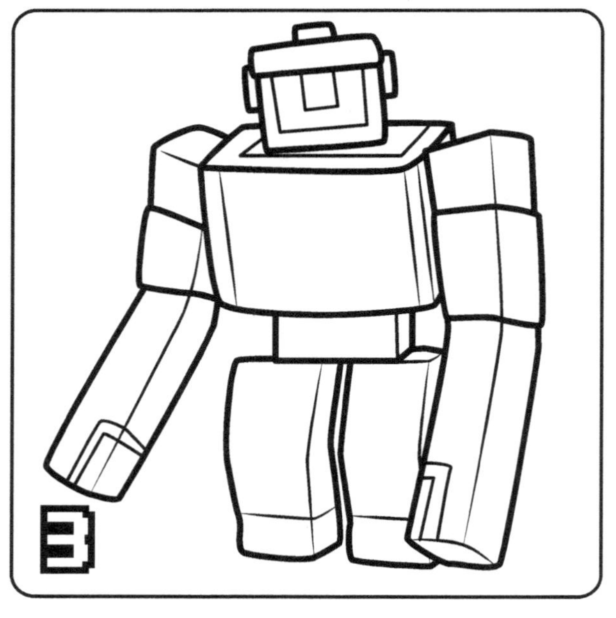

Now, it's your turn

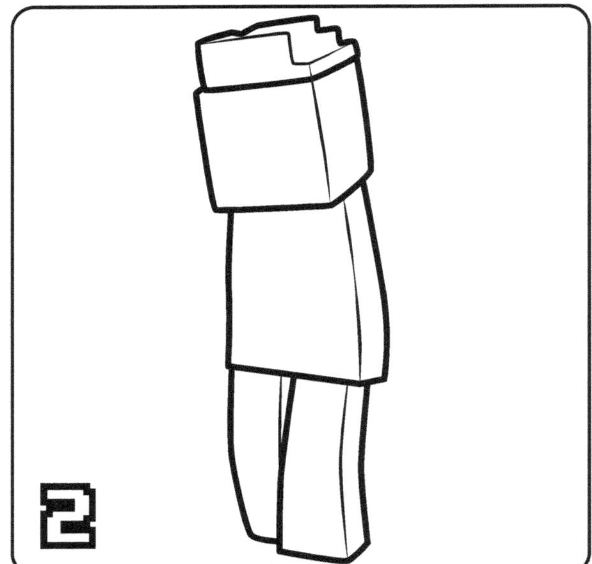

How to draw?
VAL

Now, it's your turn

WILLY

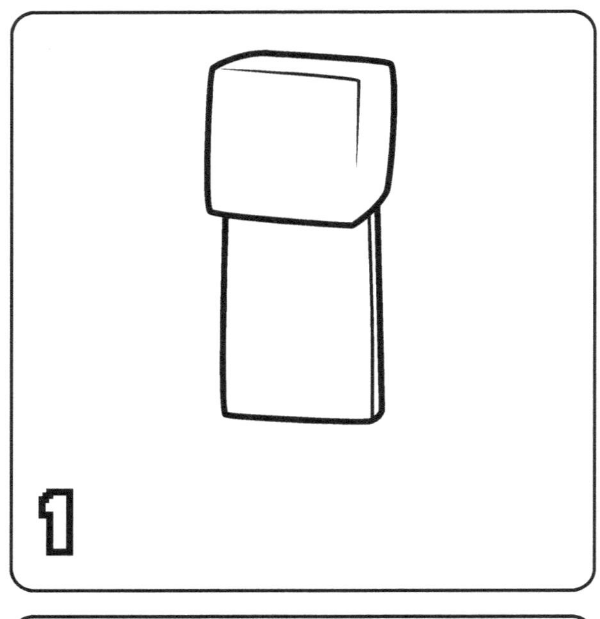

1

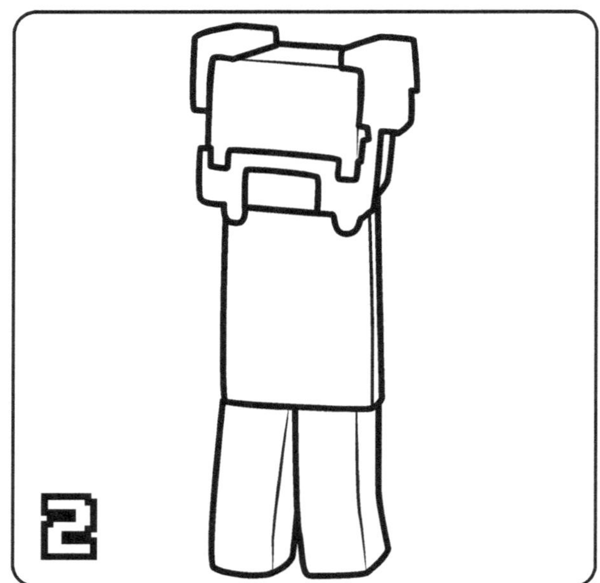

2

3

4

Now, it's your turn

How to draw?
TERRY

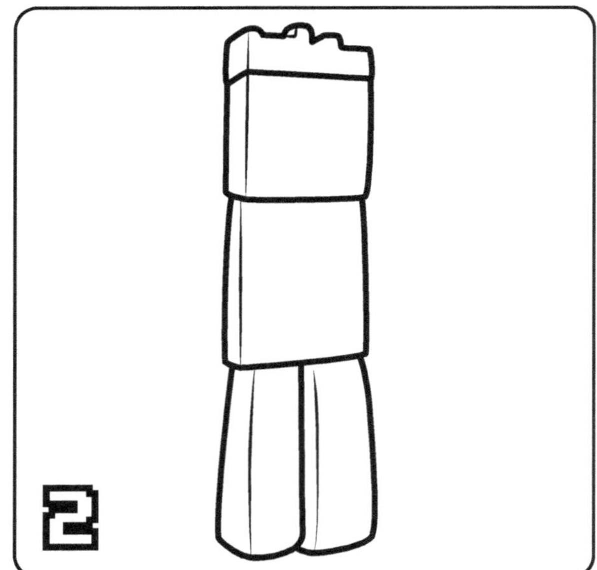

Now, it's your turn

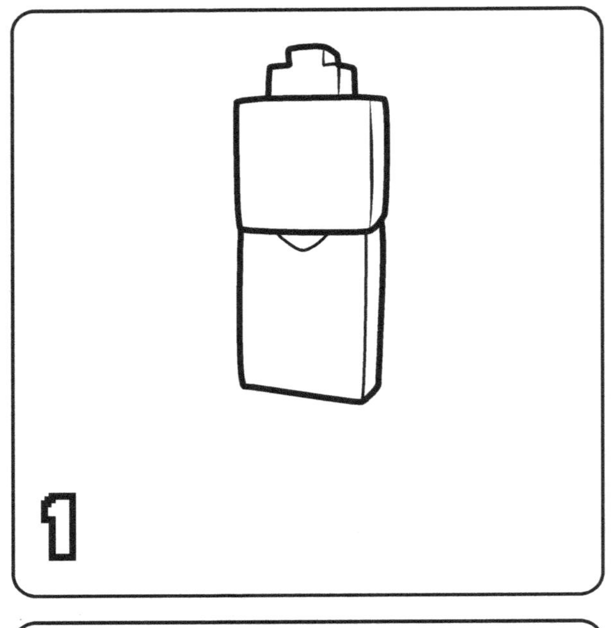

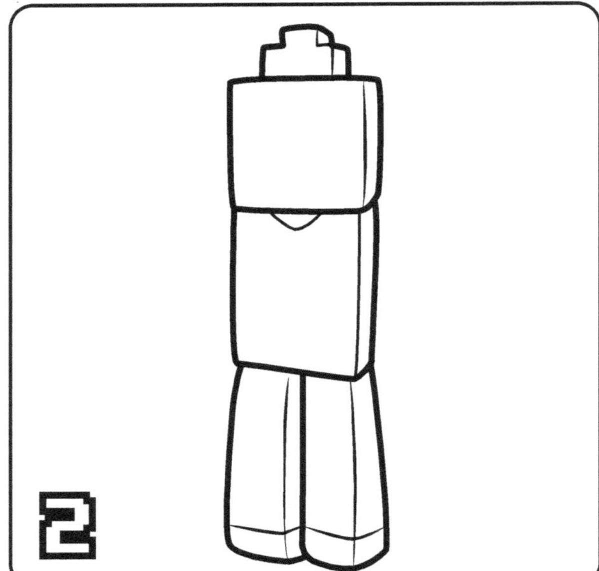

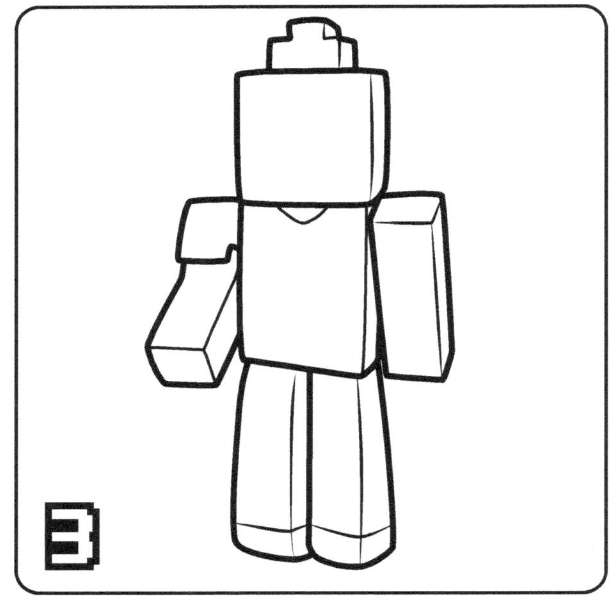

How to draw?
SOUP

Now, it's your turn

How to draw?
BINTA

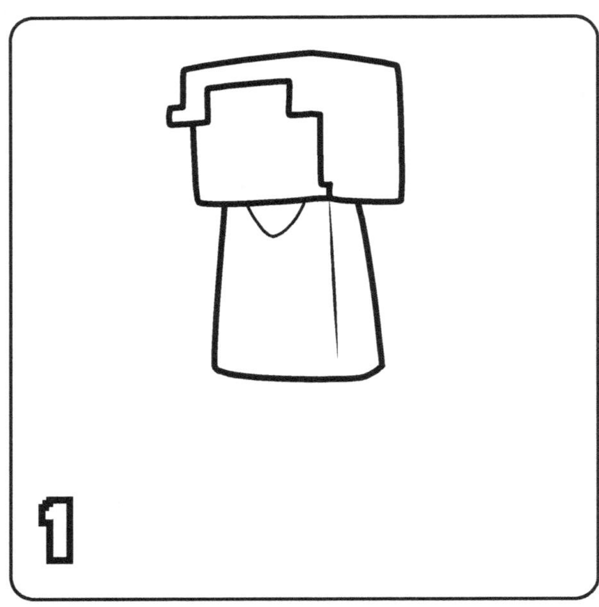

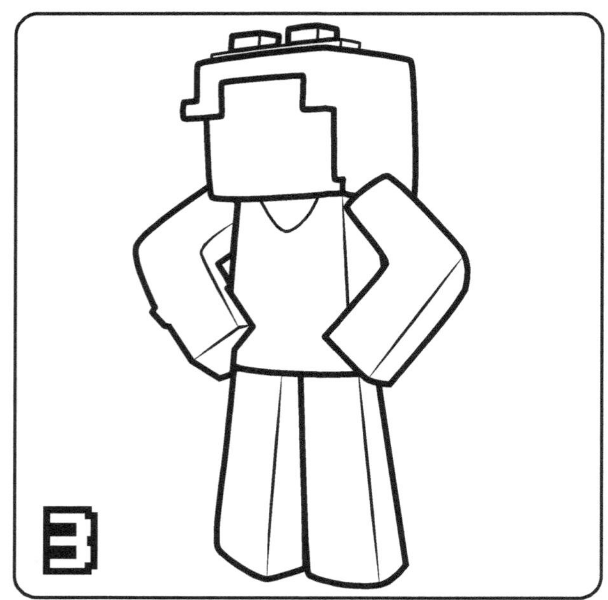

Now, it's your turn

How to draw?
DXBLOOD

1

2

3

4

Now, it's your turn

How to draw?
KENT

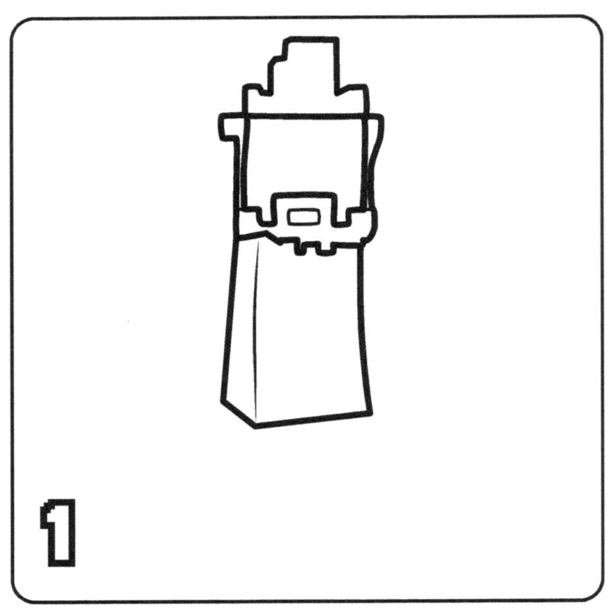

Now, it's your turn

How to draw?
WARDEN

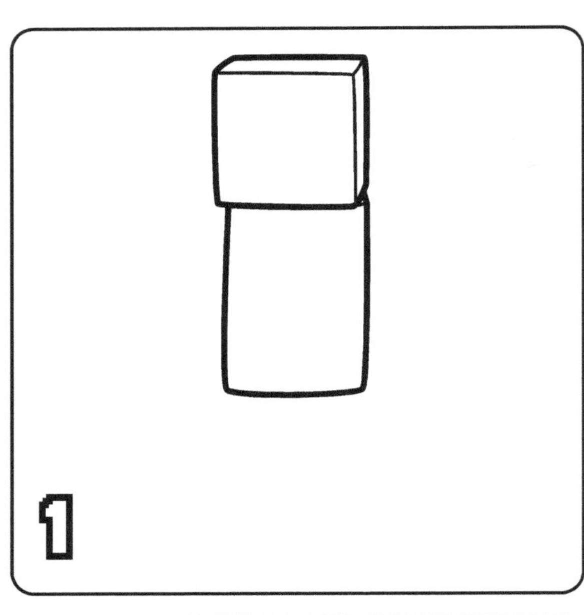

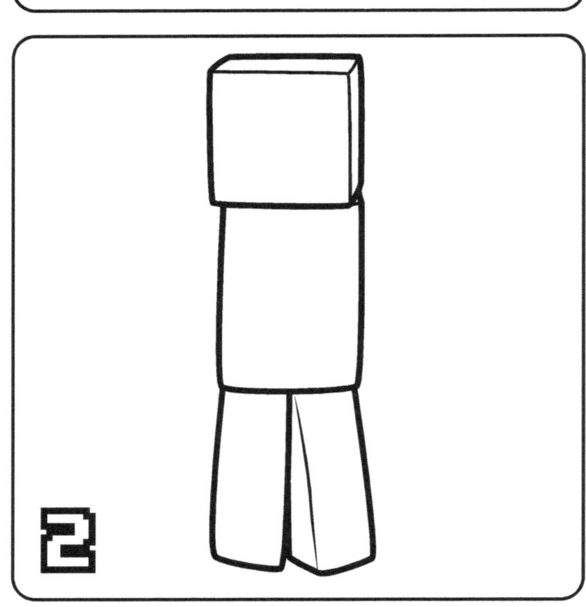

Now, it's your turn

How to draw?
PETRA

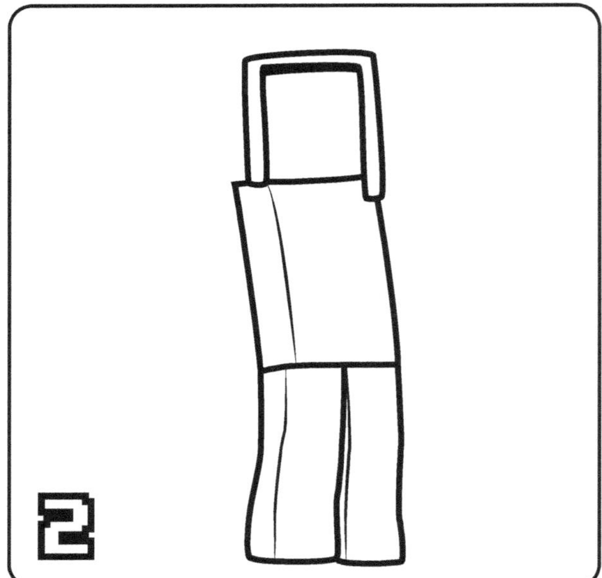

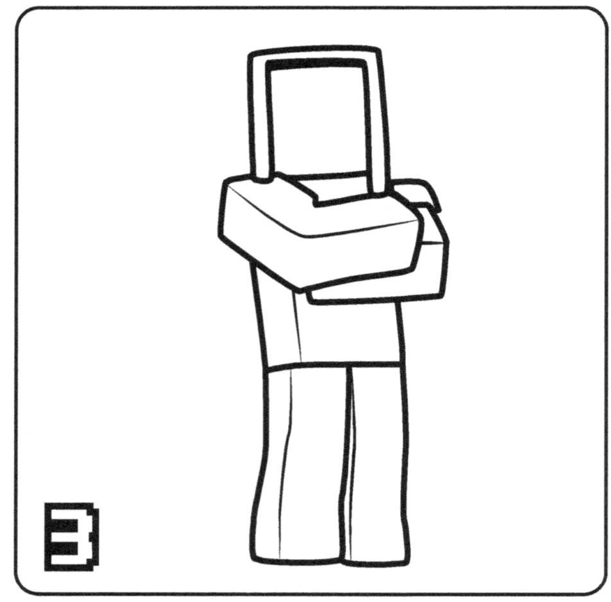

Now, it's your turn

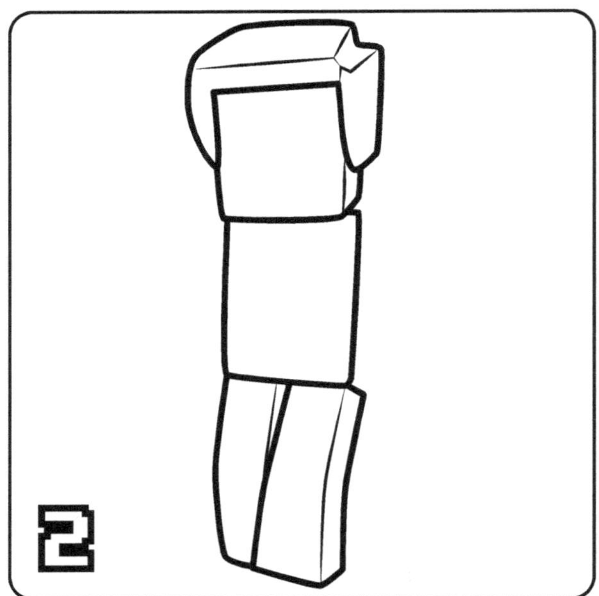

How to draw?
ROB

Now, it's your turn

How to draw?
WOLVEN

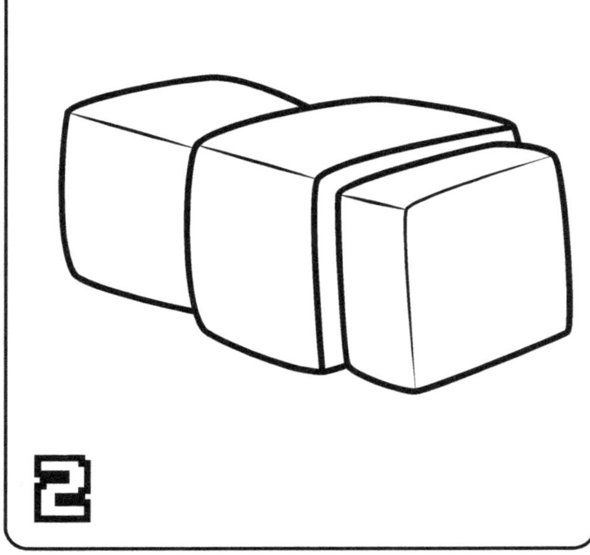

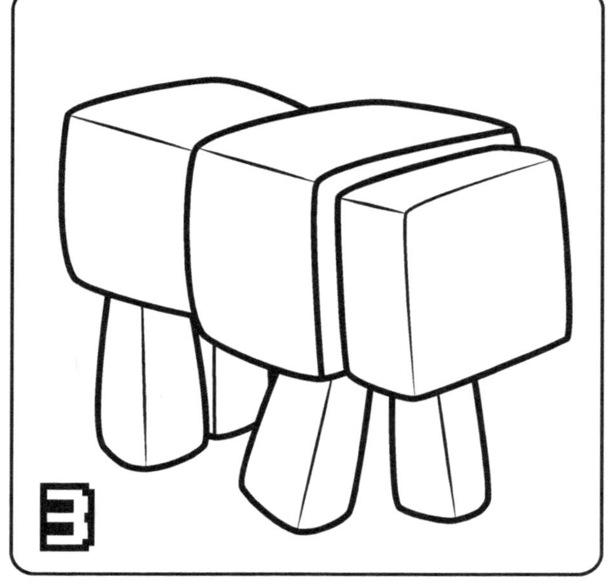

Now, it's your turn

JEWEL

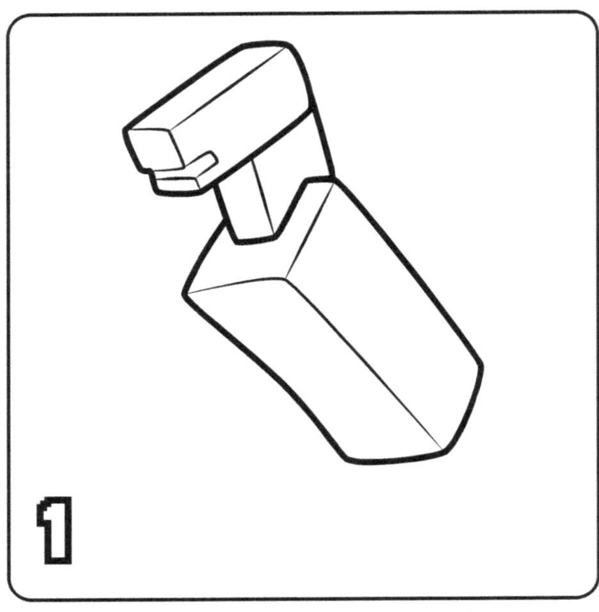

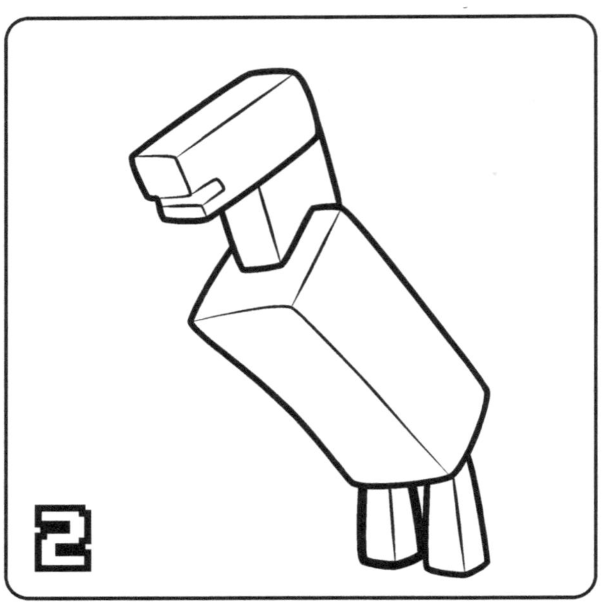

Now, it's your turn

How to draw?
STACY

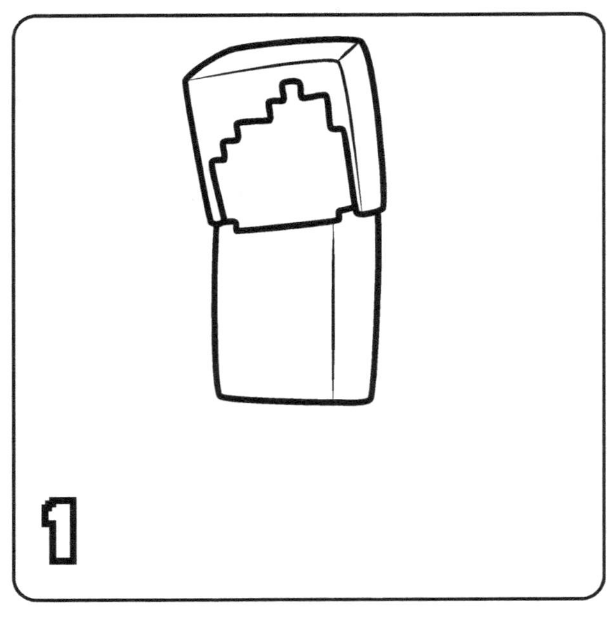

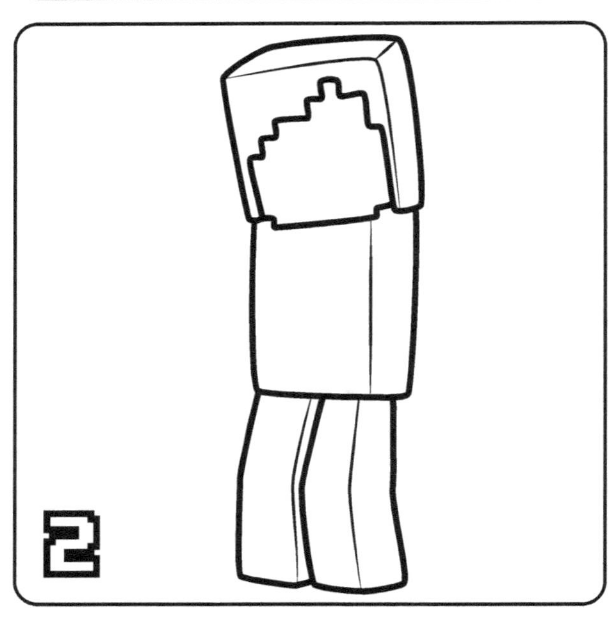

Now, it's your turn

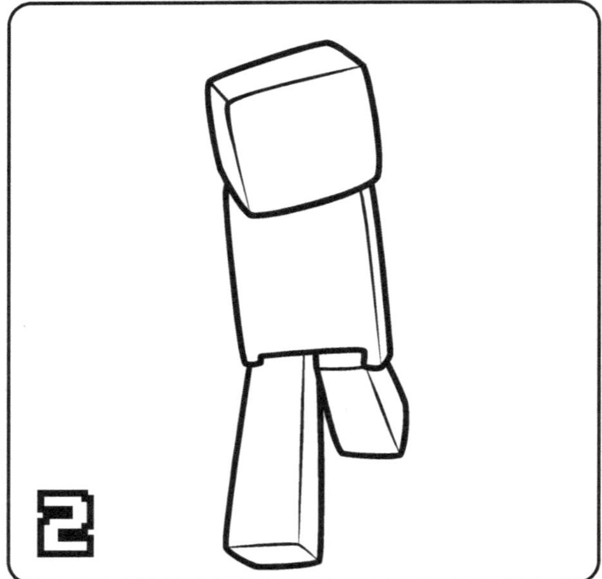

How to draw?
ALEX

Now, it's your turn

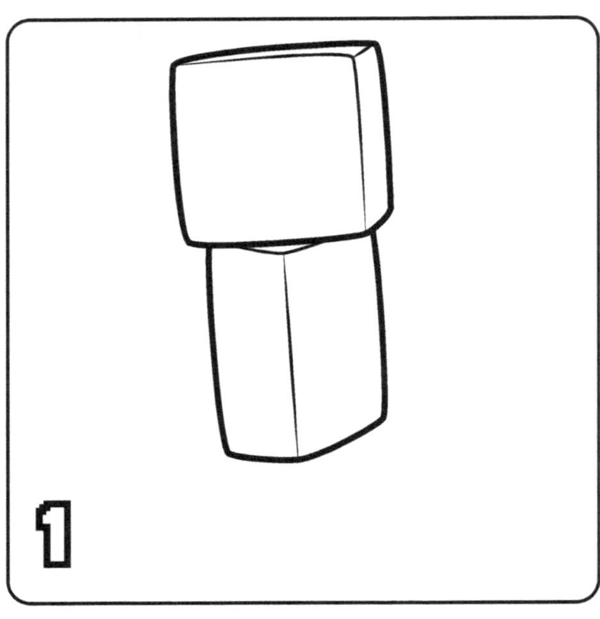

1

How to draw?
CREPPER

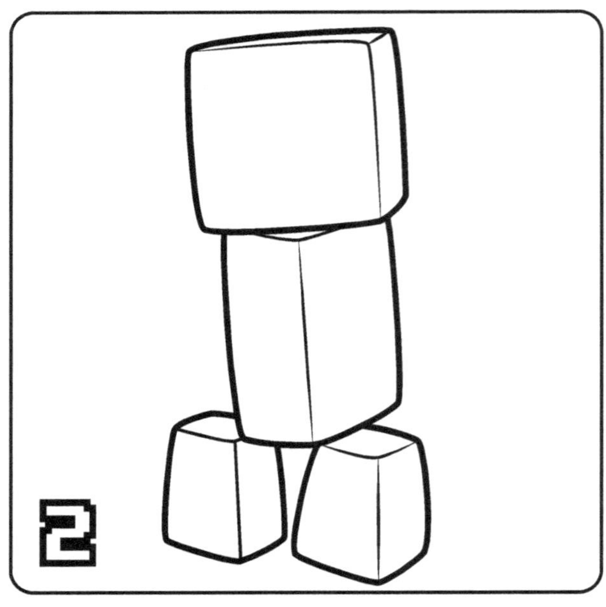

2

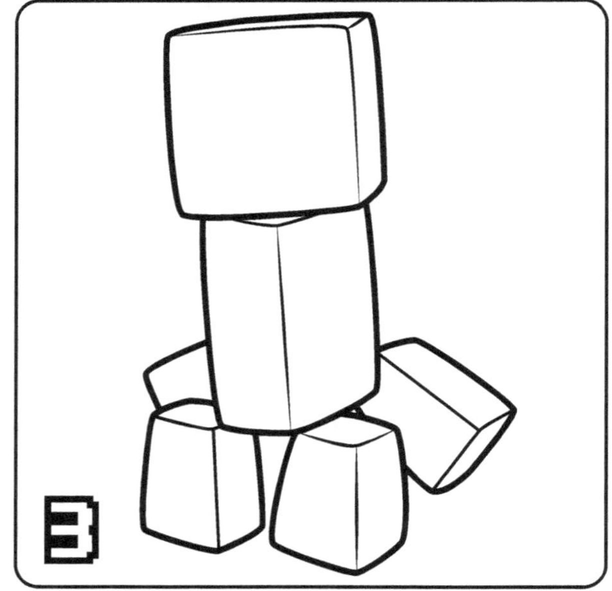

3

4

Now, it's your turn

How to draw?
DHAND

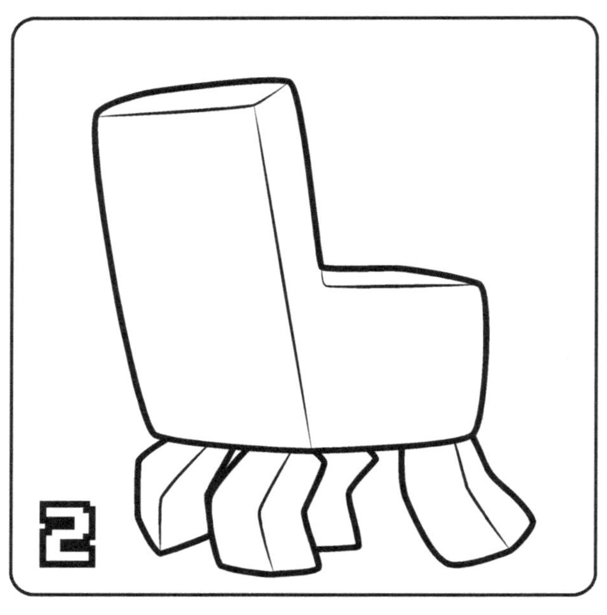

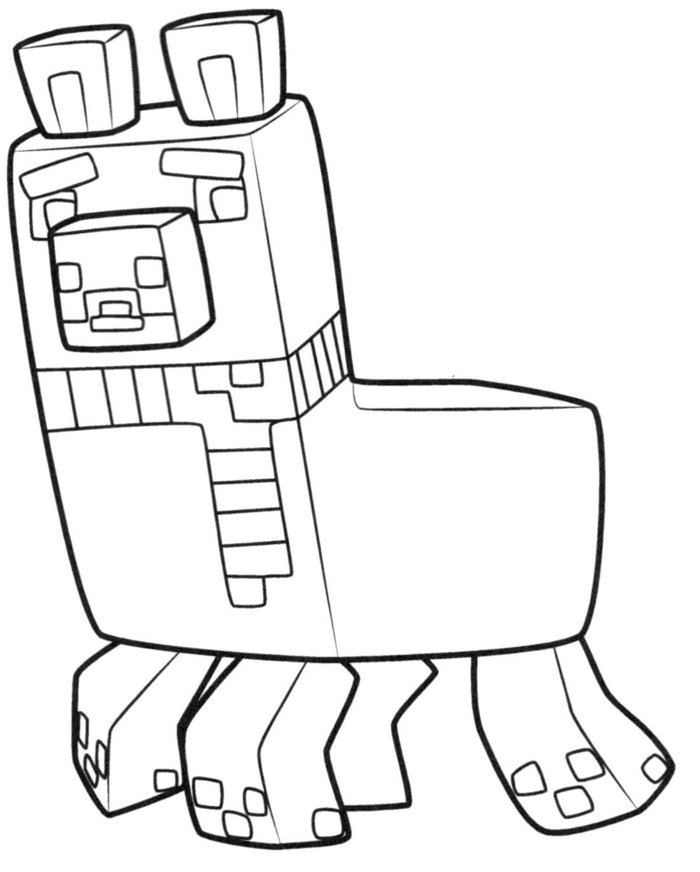

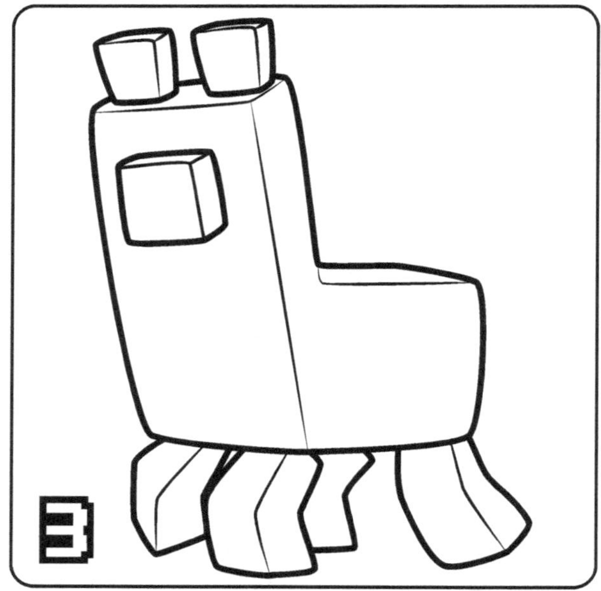

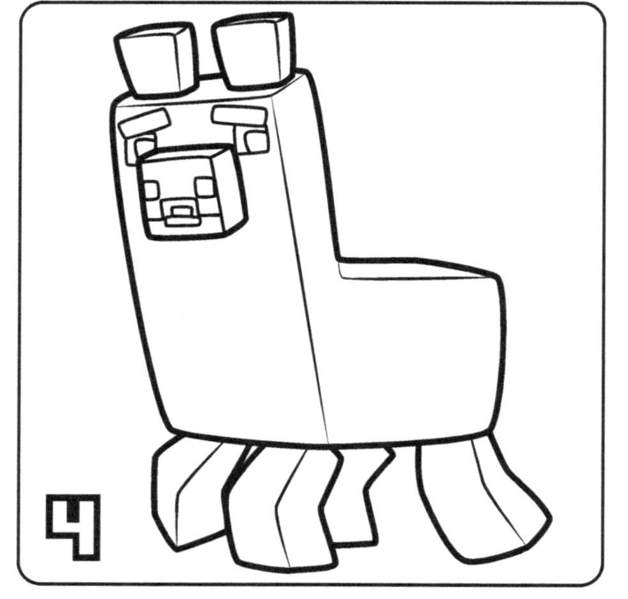

Now, it's your turn

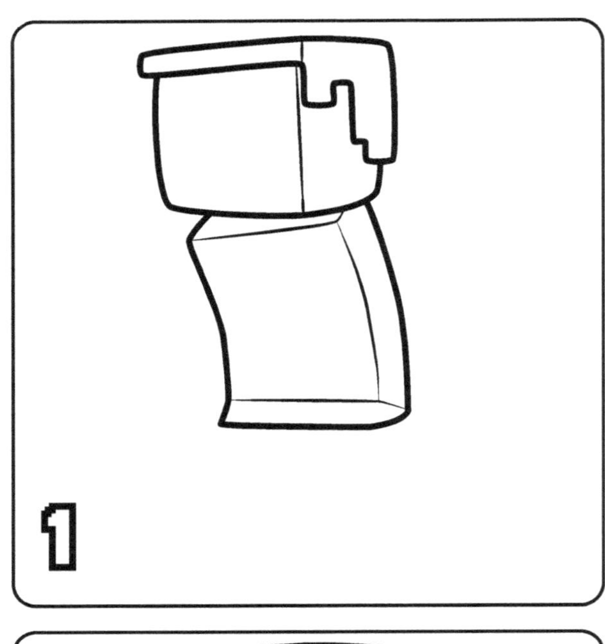

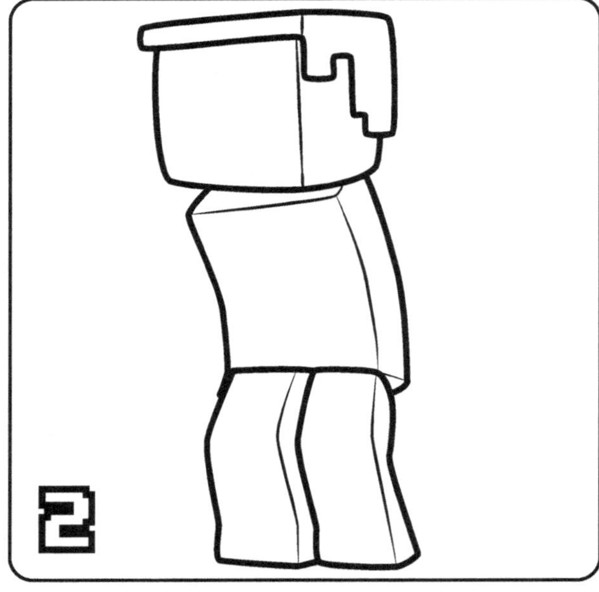

How to draw?
GILL

Now, it's your turn

ZOMBIE

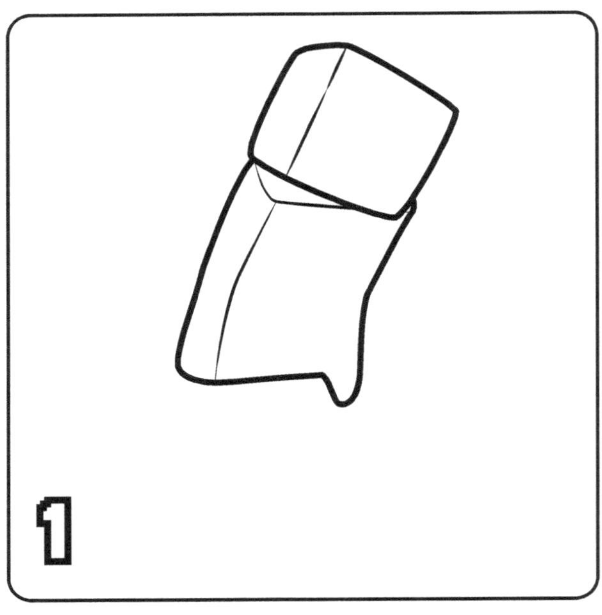

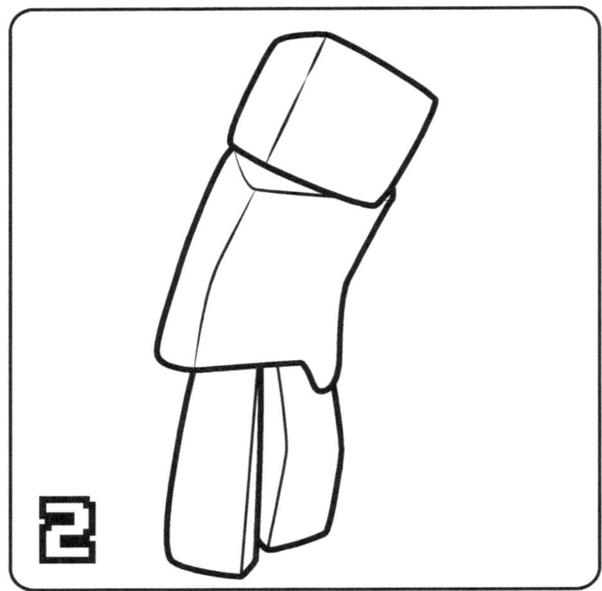

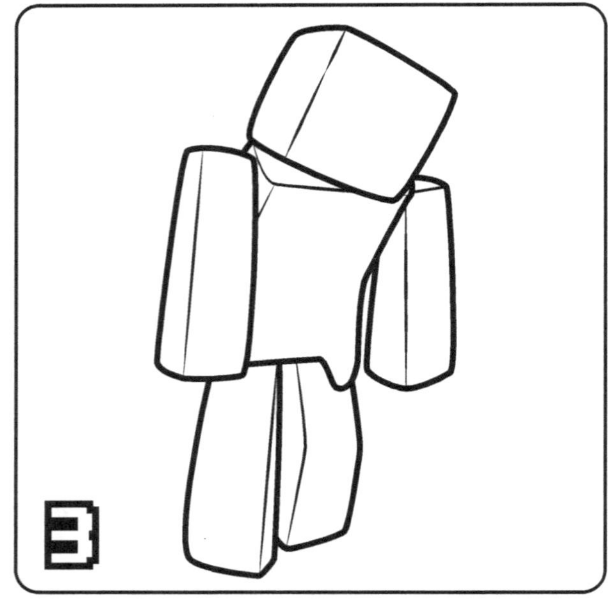

Now, it's your turn

GABRIEL

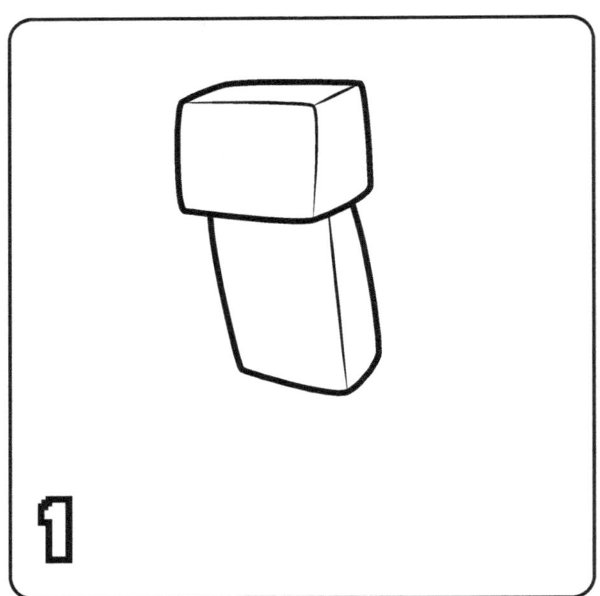

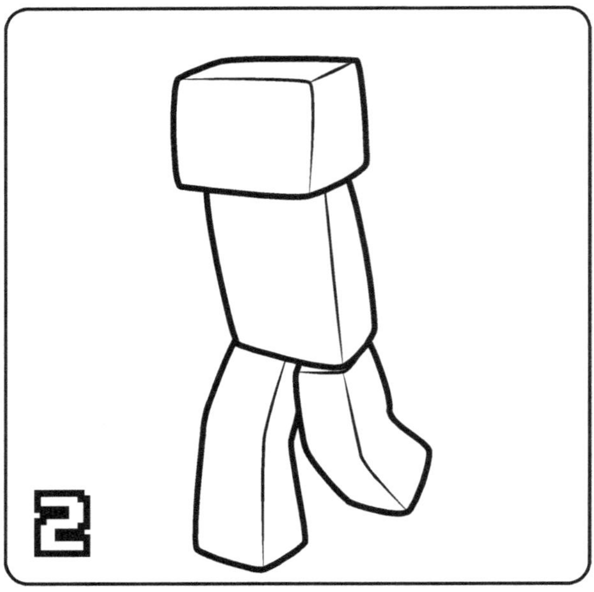

Now, it's your turn

How to draw?
REUBEN

1

2

3

4

Now, it's your turn

DLIVIA

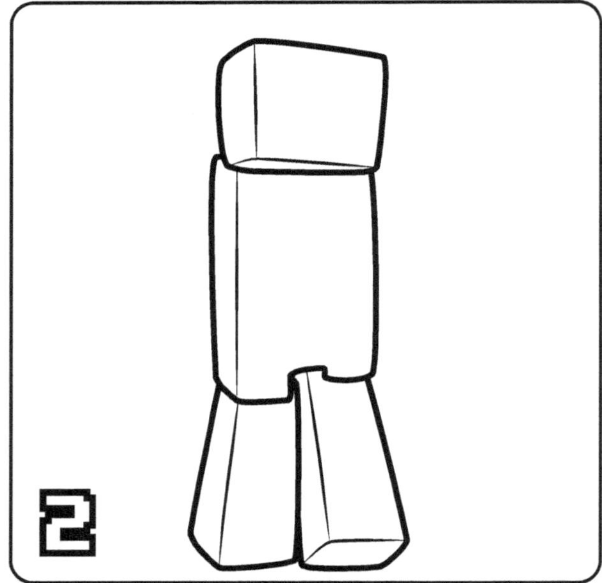

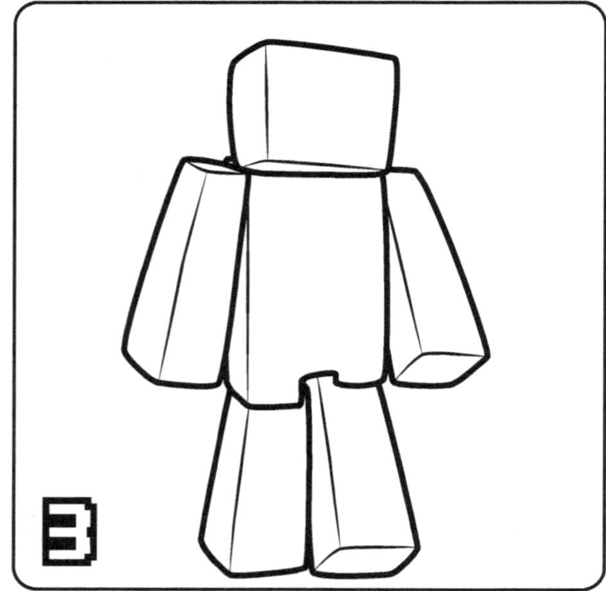

Now, it's your turn

1

How to draw?
BRICK

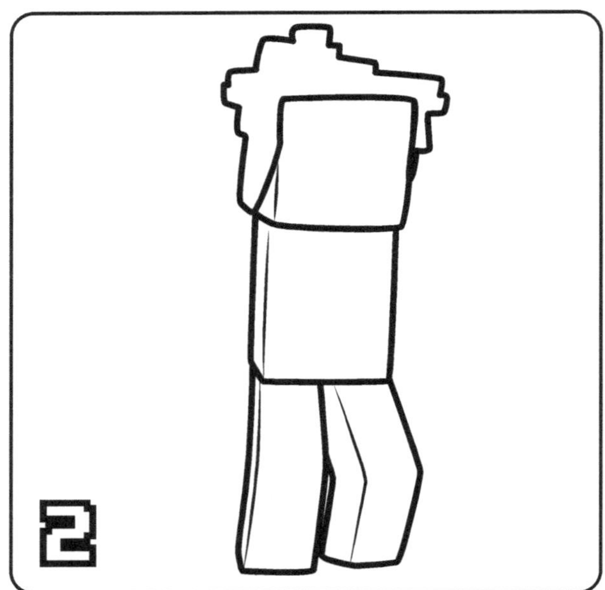

2

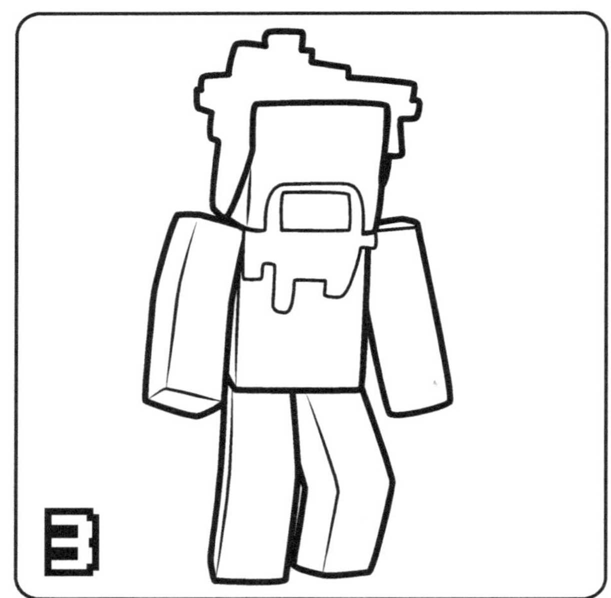

3

4

Now, it's your turn

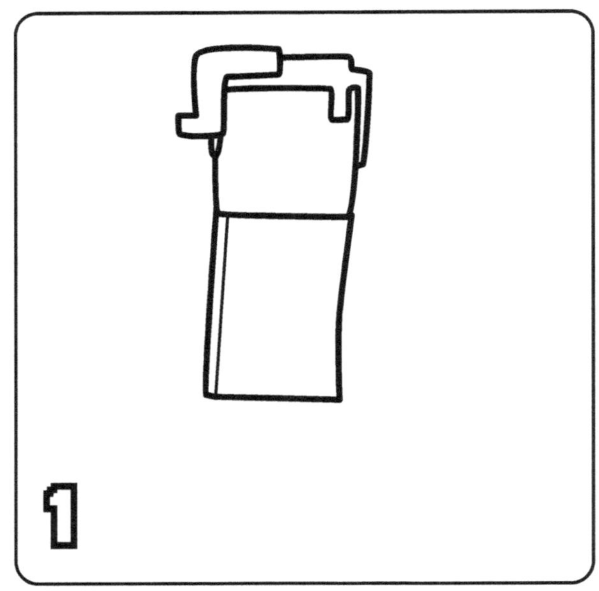

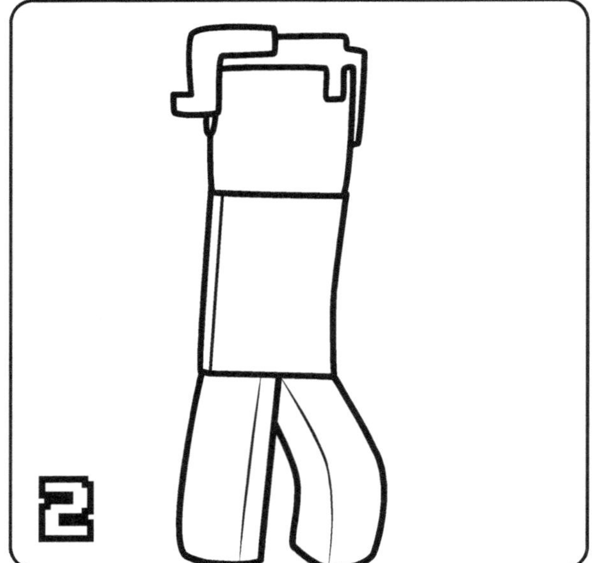

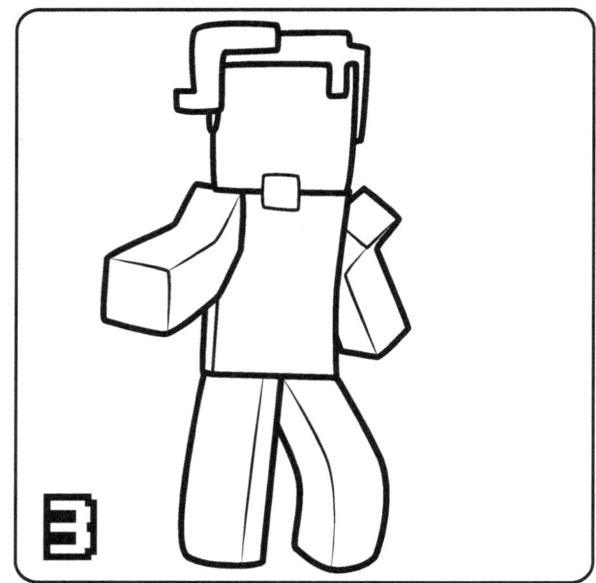

How to draw?
ROMEO

Now, it's your turn

ANTHONY

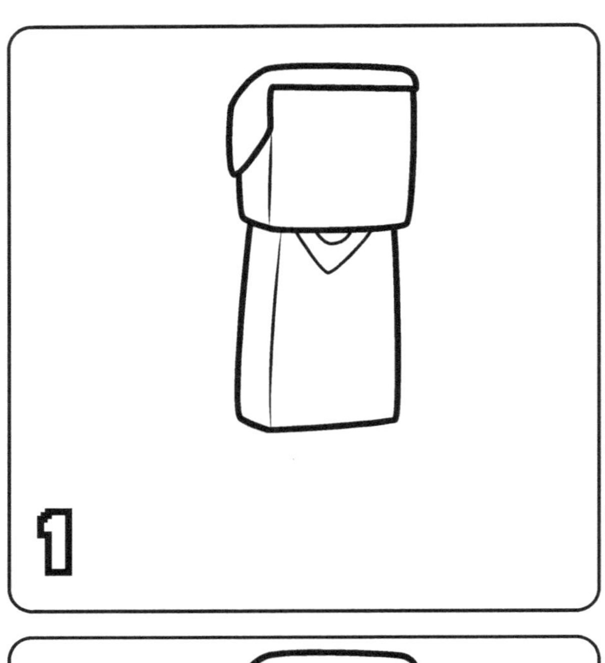

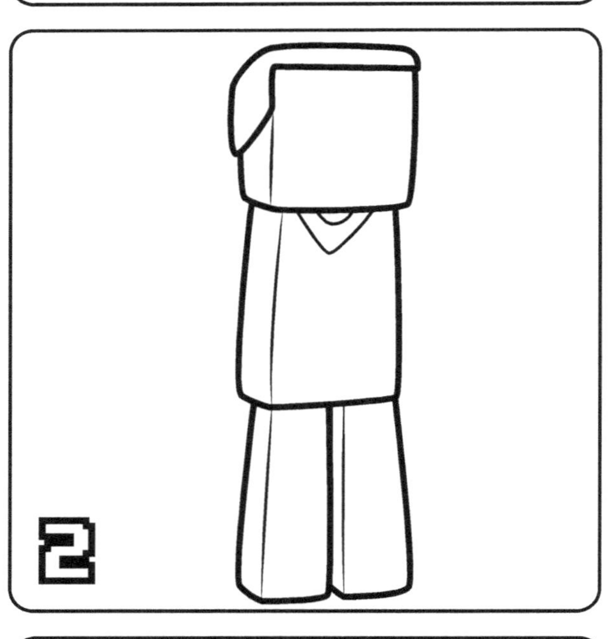

Now, it's your turn

Now, it's your turn

How to draw?
VOS

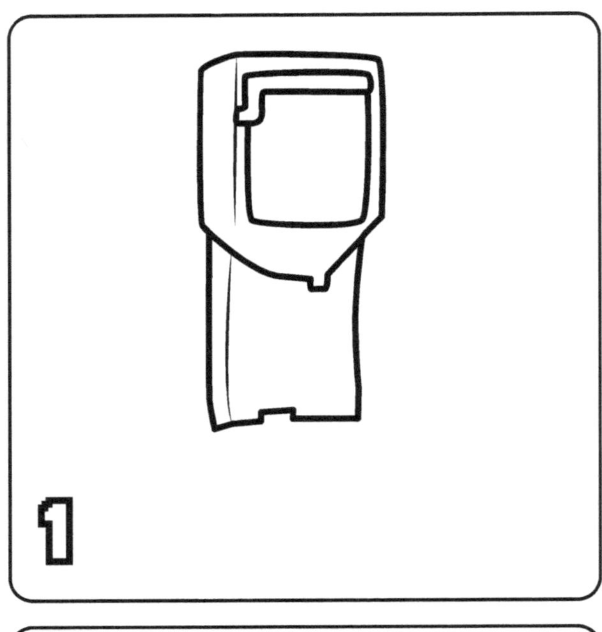

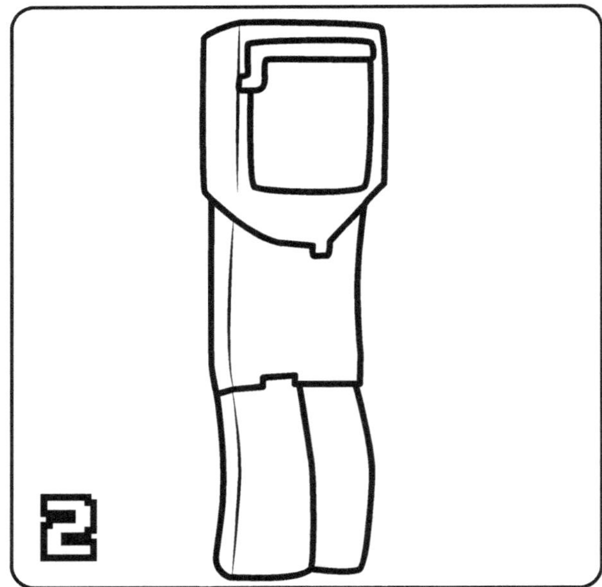

Now, it's your turn

How to draw?
NURM

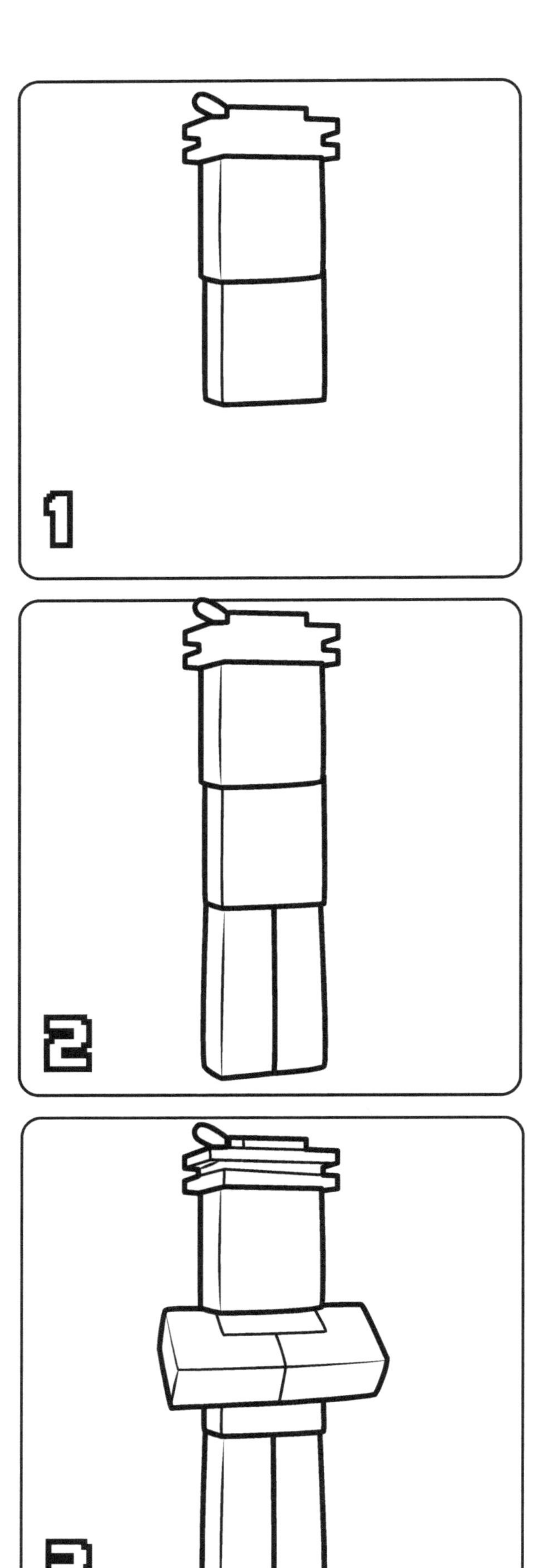

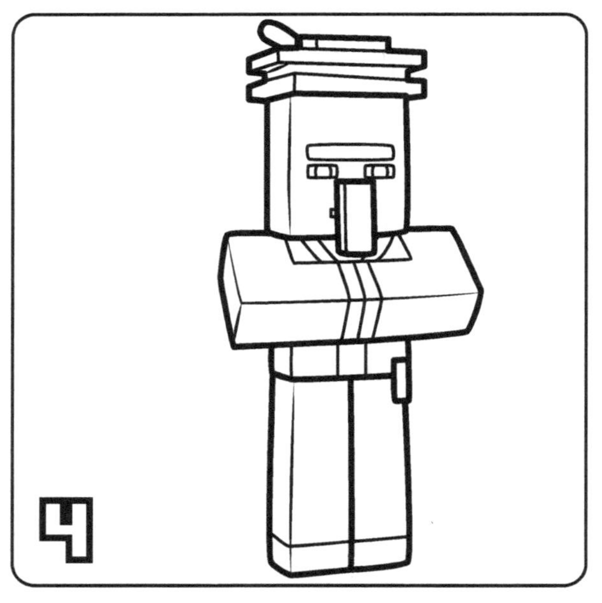

Now, it's your turn

Now, it's your turn

How to draw?
Zombie Villager Baby

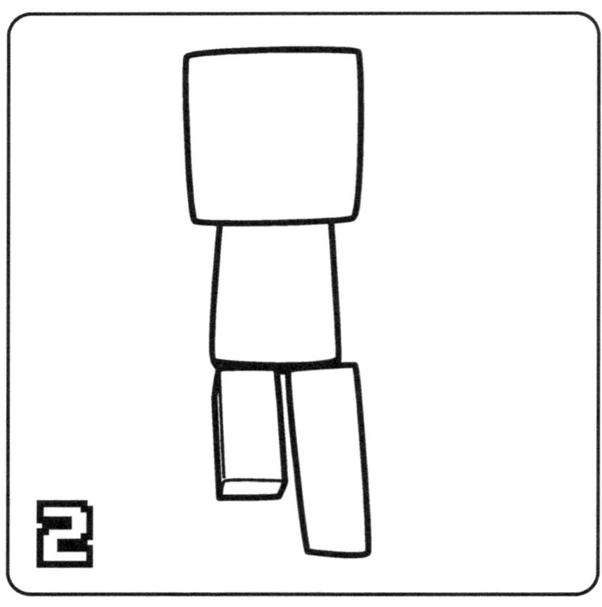

Now, it's your turn

How to draw?
GEOMANCER

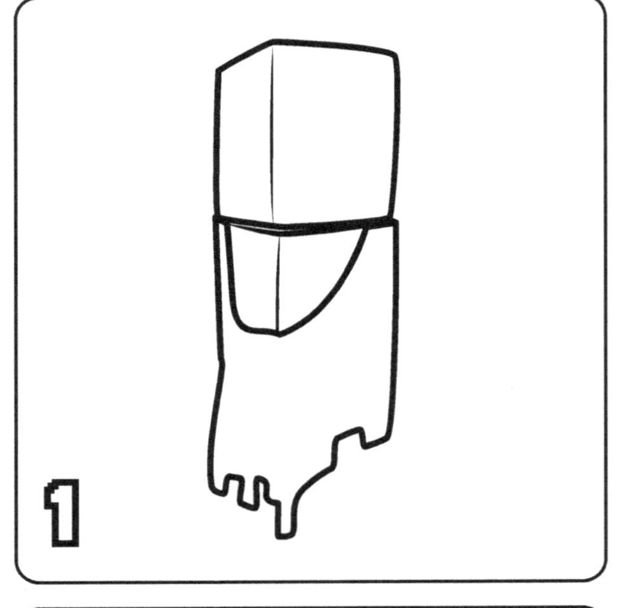

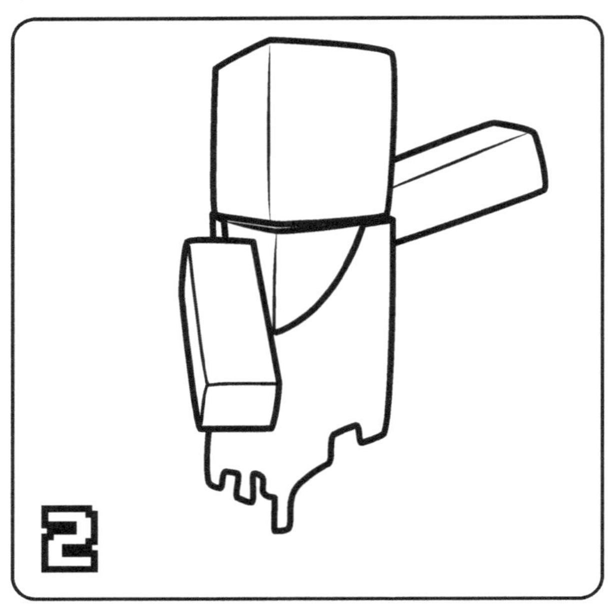

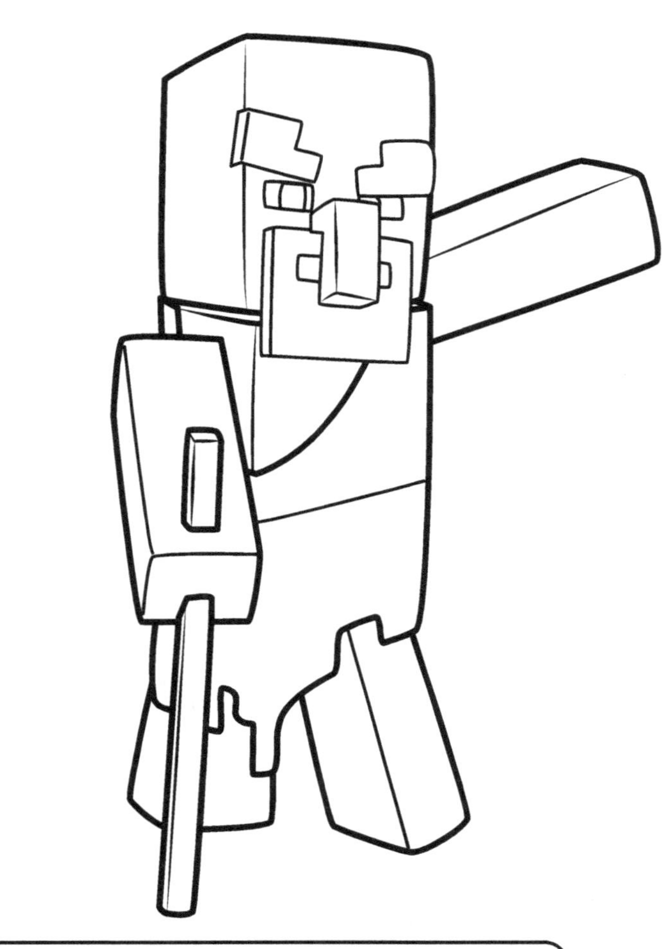

Now, it's your turn

How to draw?
XARA

1

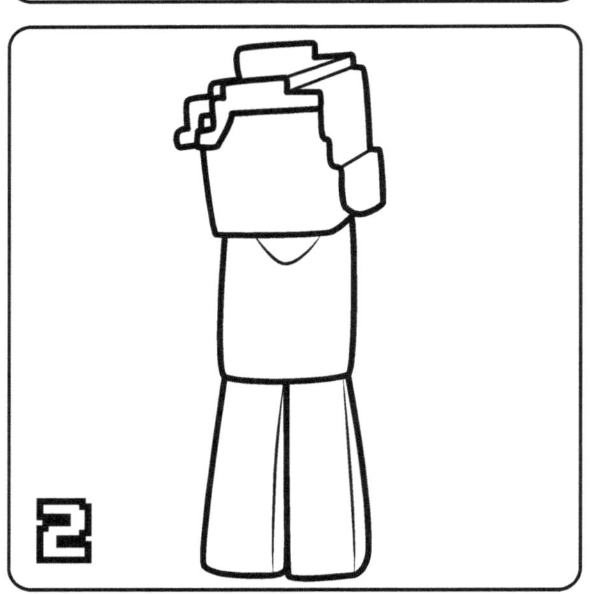

2

3

4

Now, it's your turn

How to draw?
JACK

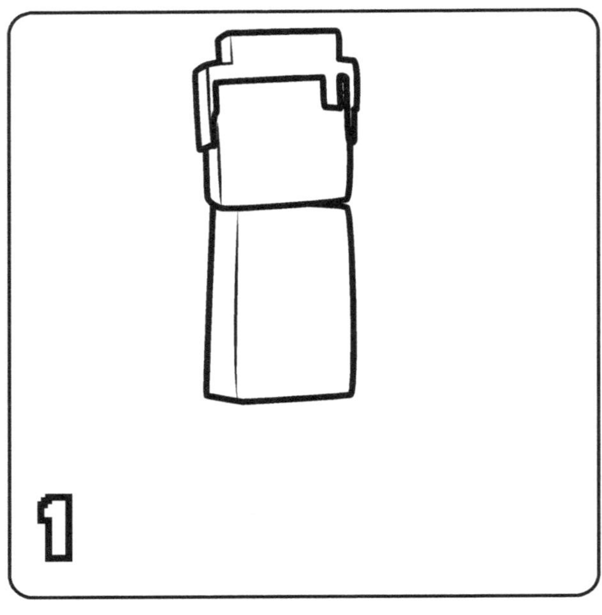

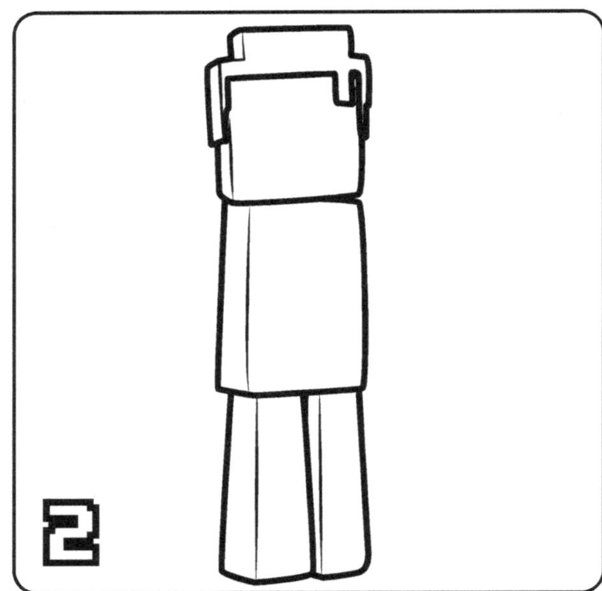

Now, it's your turn

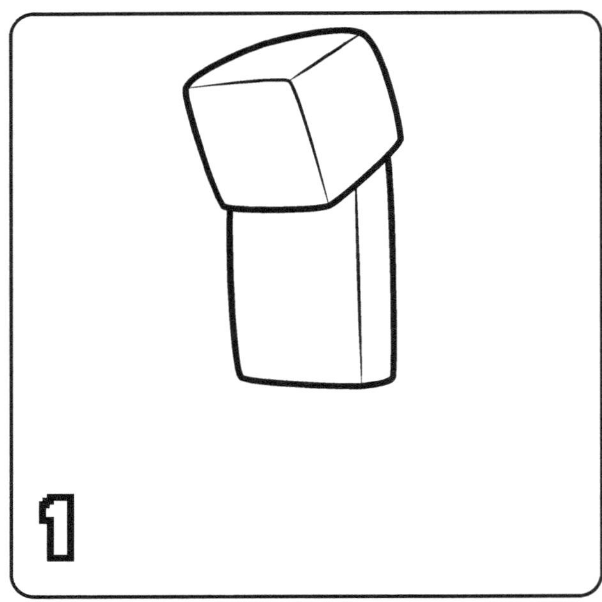

1

How to draw?
MAGNUS

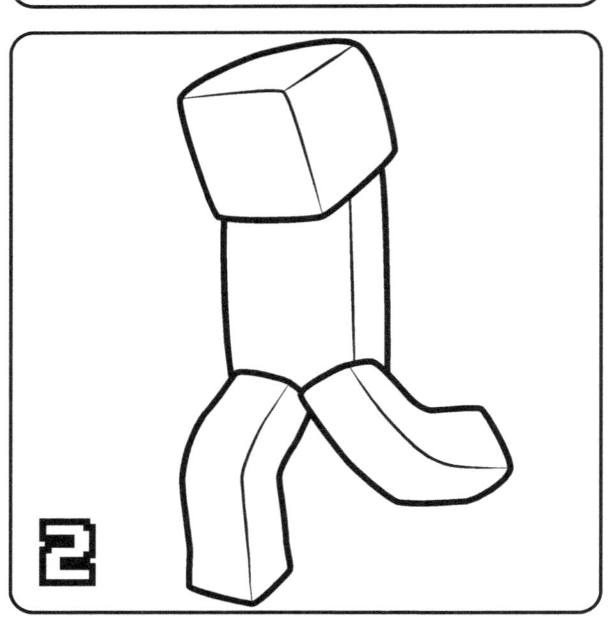

2

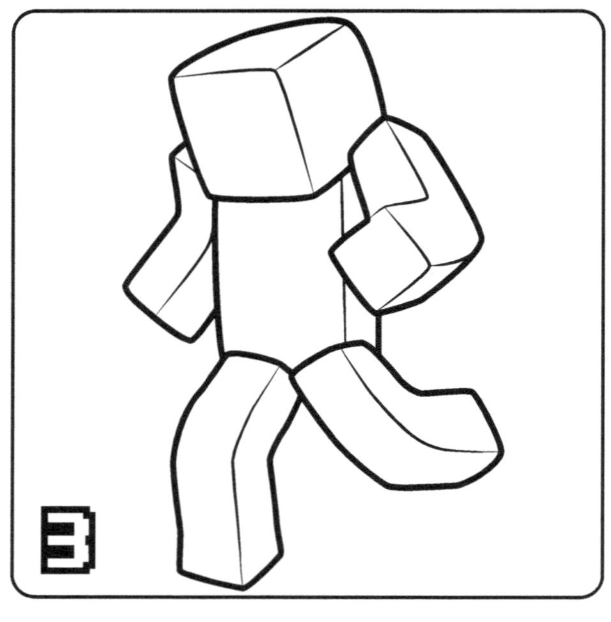

3

4

Now, it's your turn

How to draw?
ARCH ILLIGER

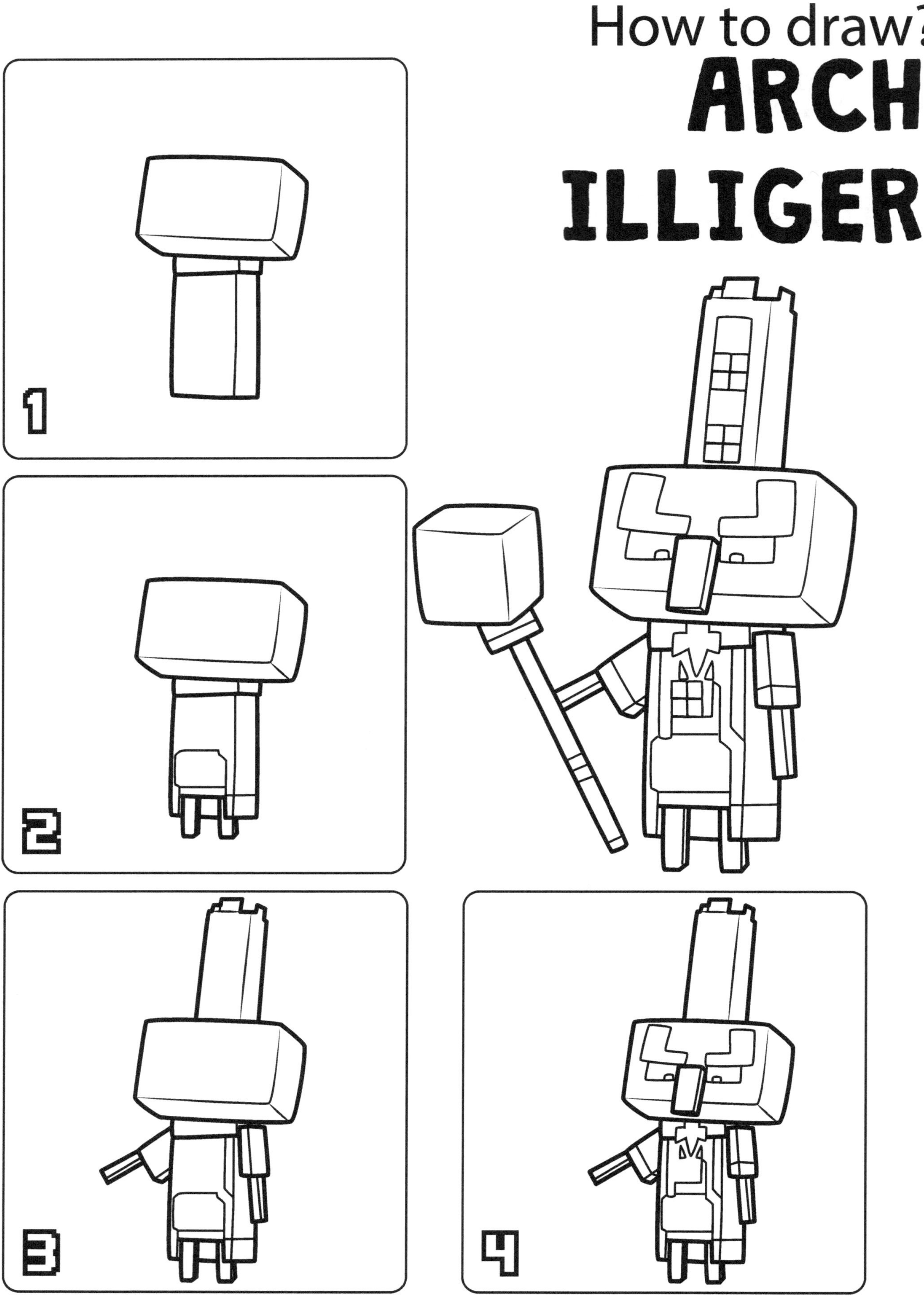

Now, it's your turn

VINDICATOR

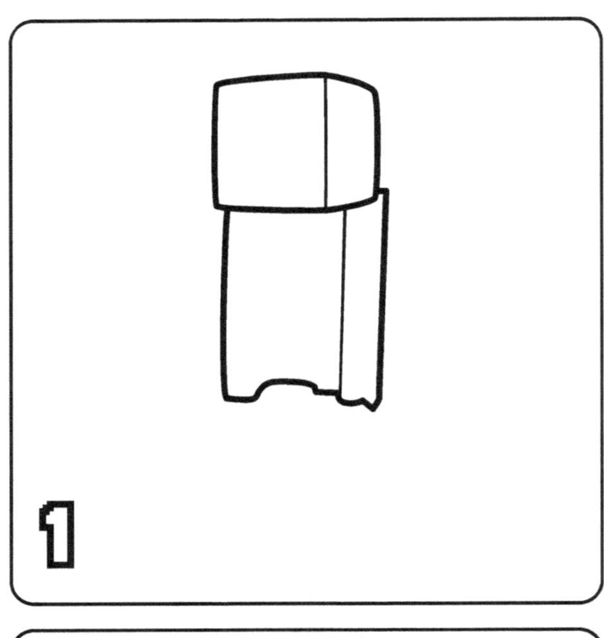

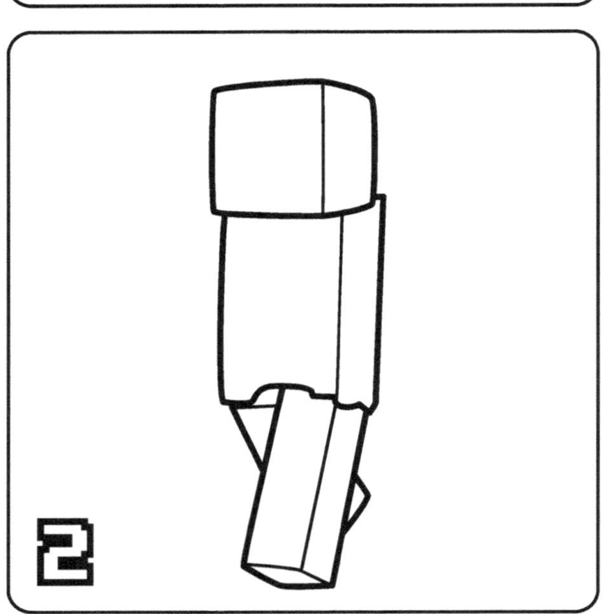

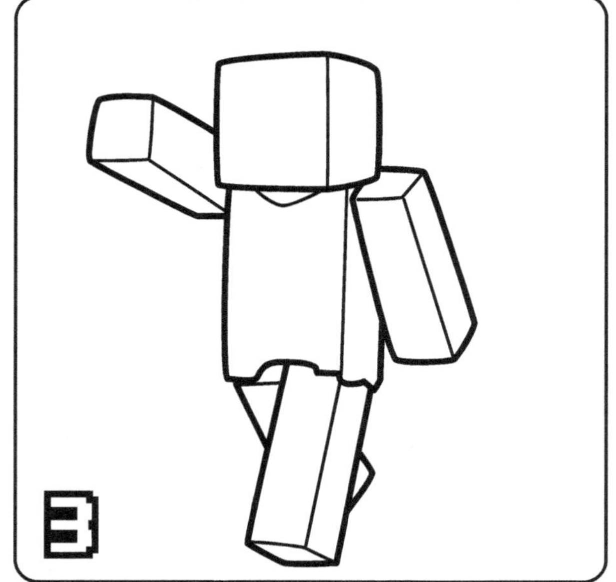

Now, it's your turn

How to draw?
STRAY

Now, it's your turn

How to draw?
SWBASTIAN

1

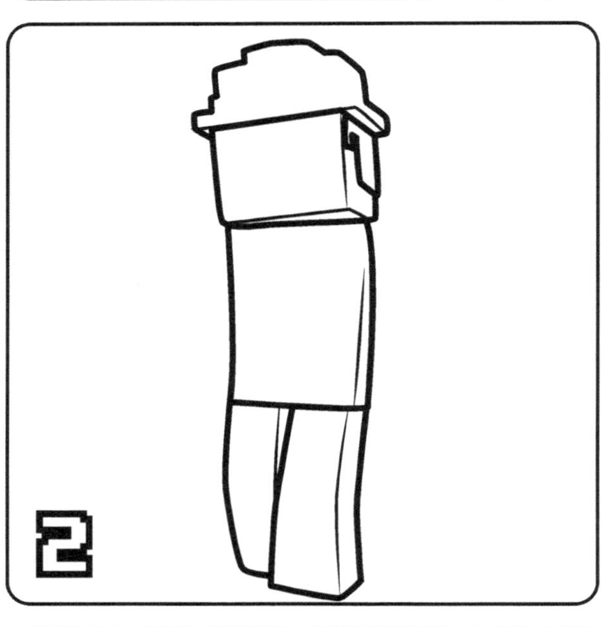

2

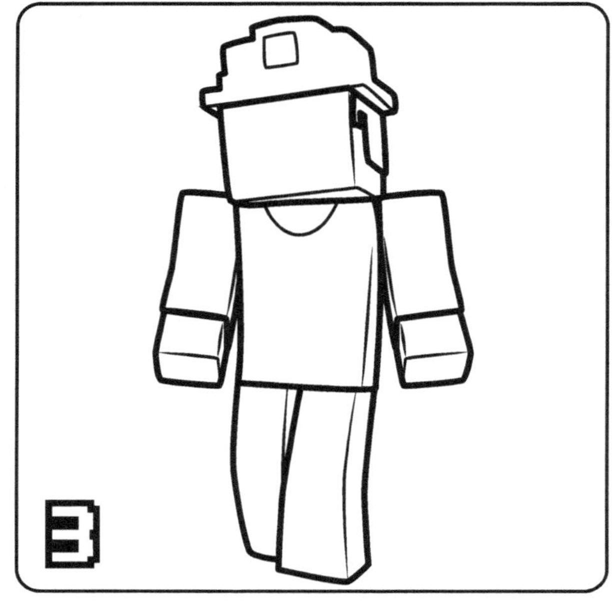

3

4

Now, it's your turn

HERZOG

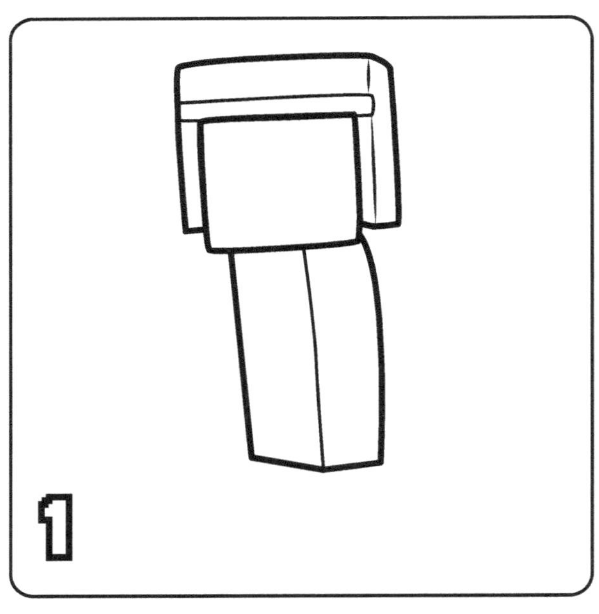

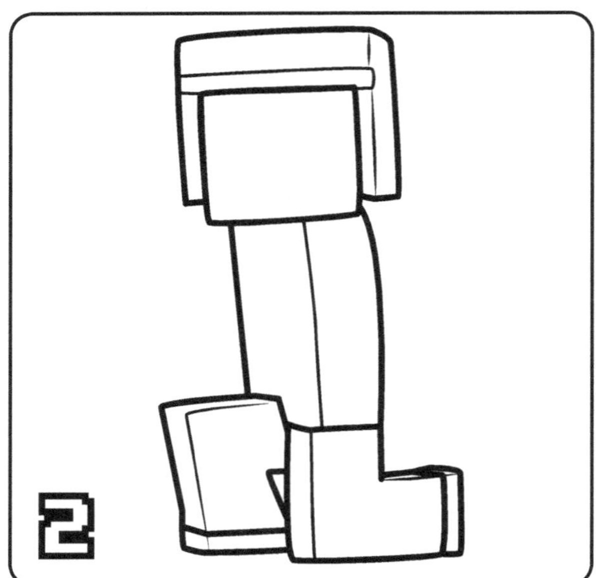

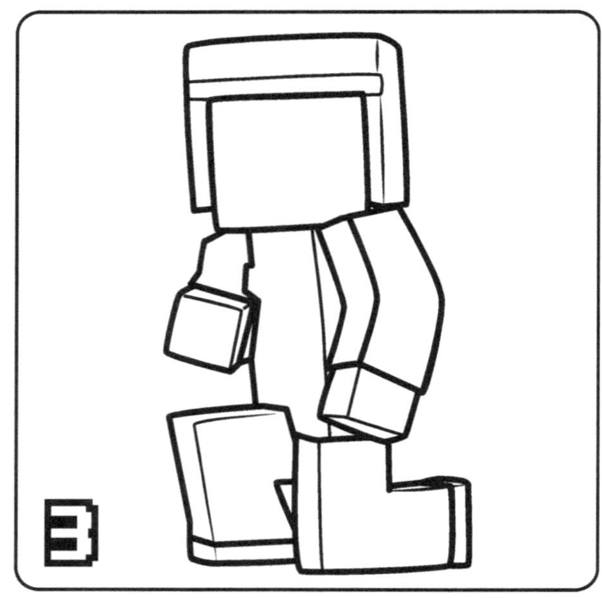

Now, it's your turn

How to draw?
IVY

1

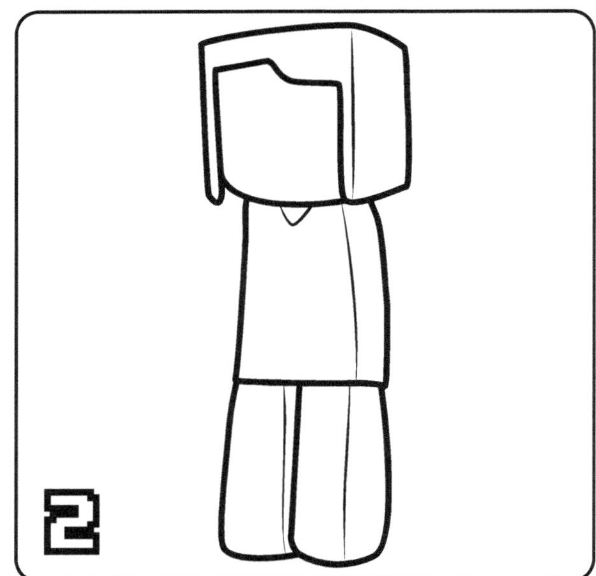

2

3

4

Now, it's your turn

How to draw?
MICKEY

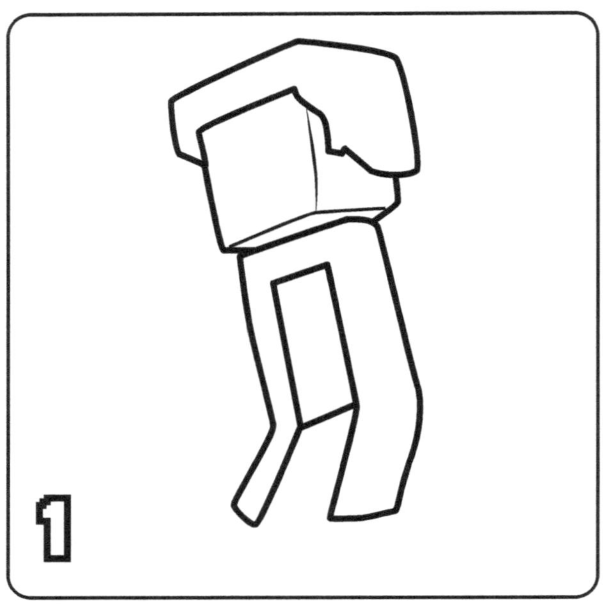

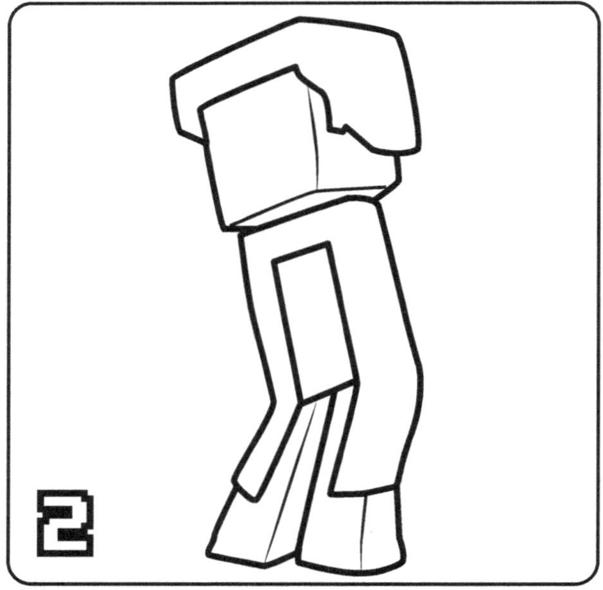

Now, it's your turn

How to draw?
WITCH

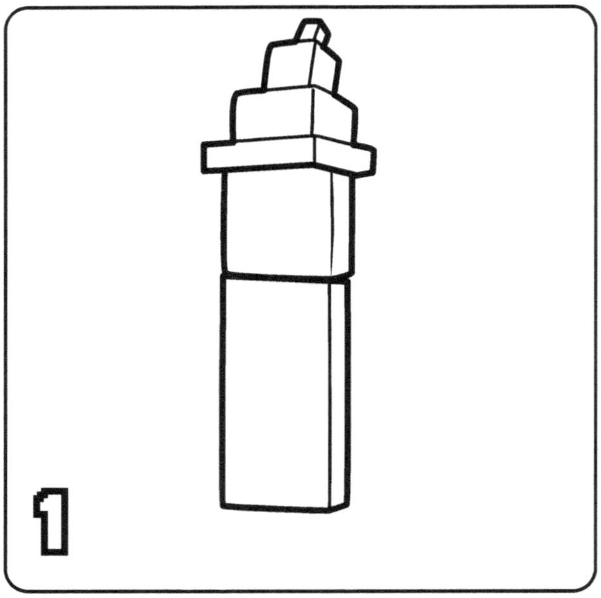

1

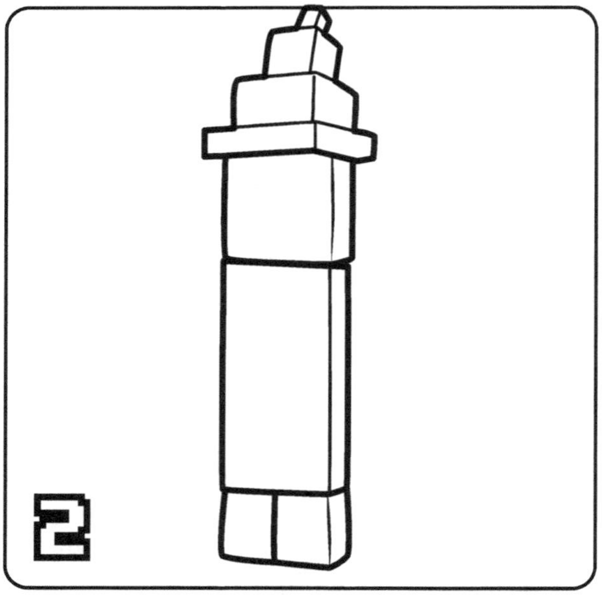

2

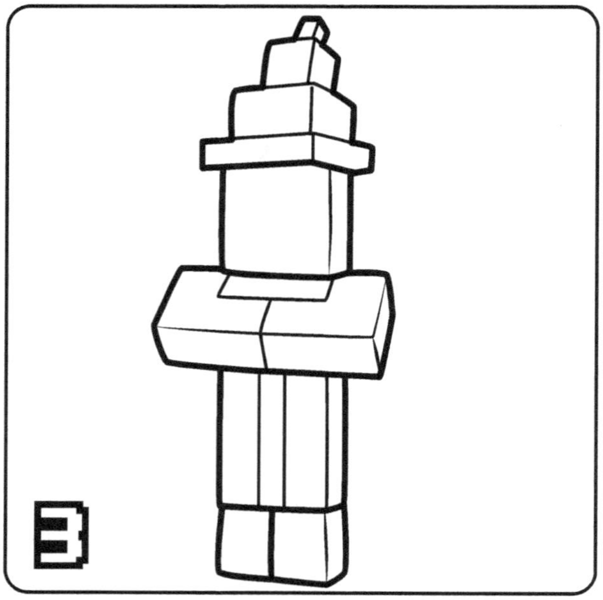

3

4

Now, it's your turn

HARPER

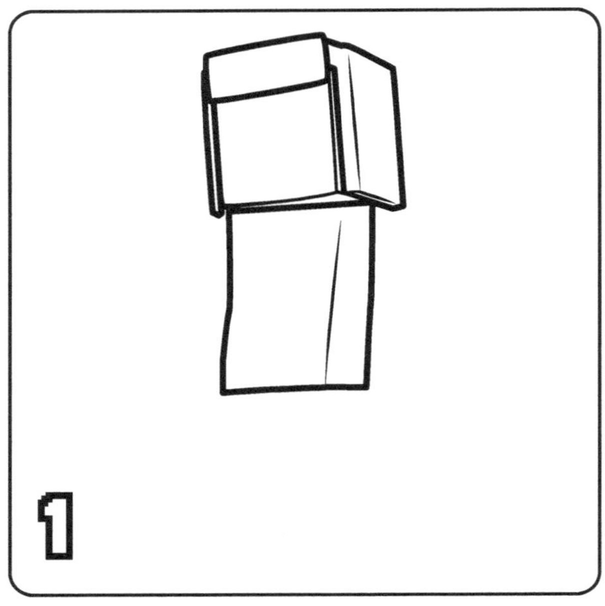

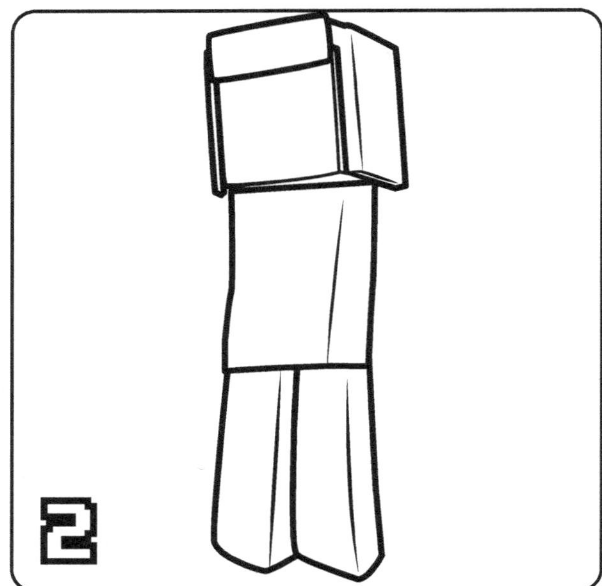

Now, it's your turn

How to draw?
MILO

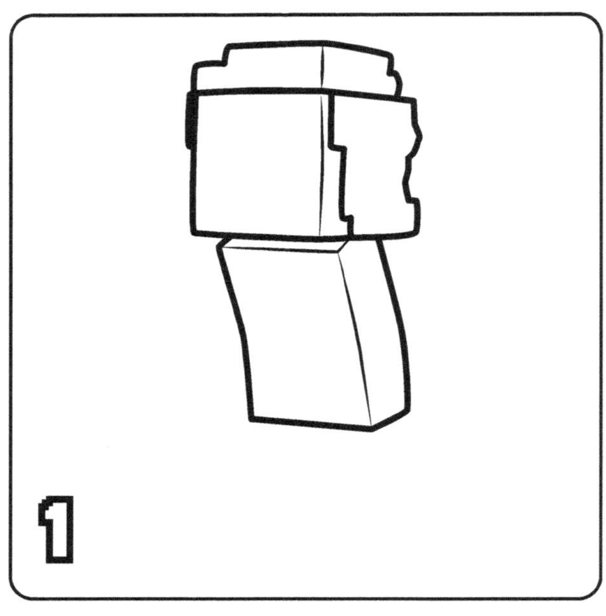

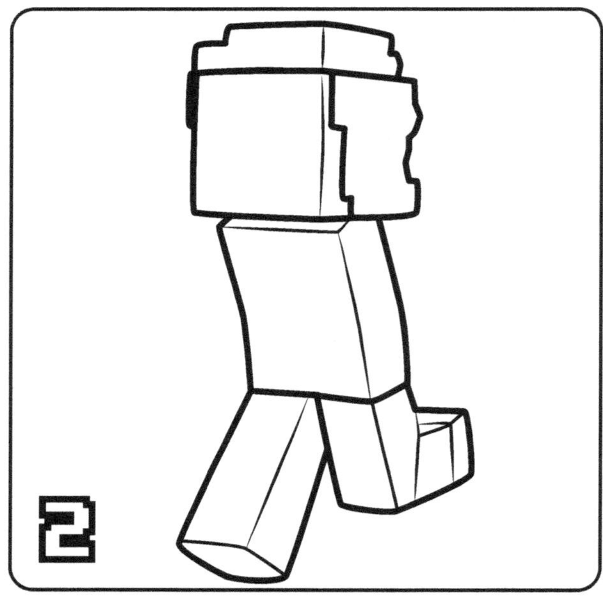

Now, it's your turn

How to draw?
DEWGON

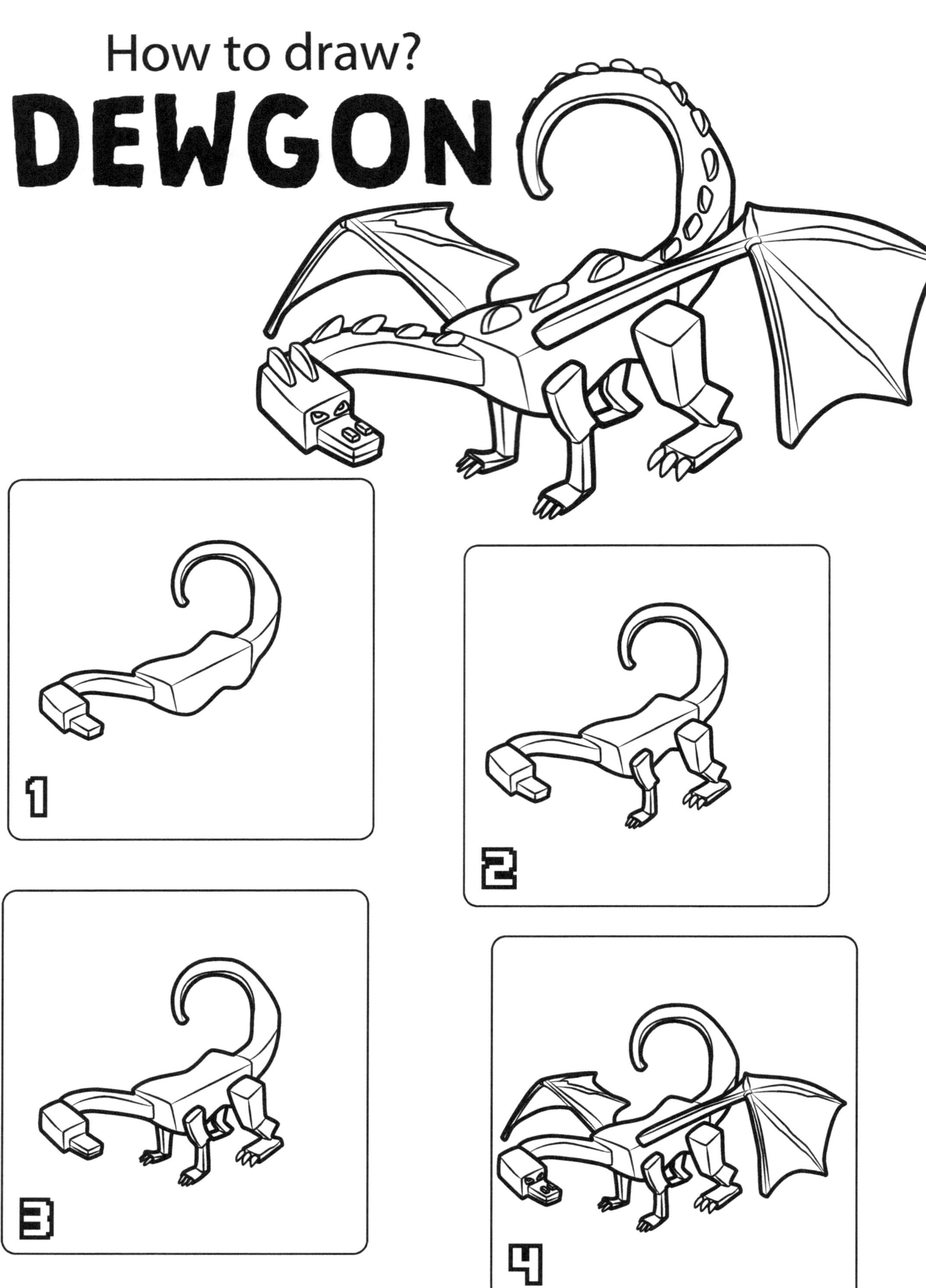

Now, it's your turn

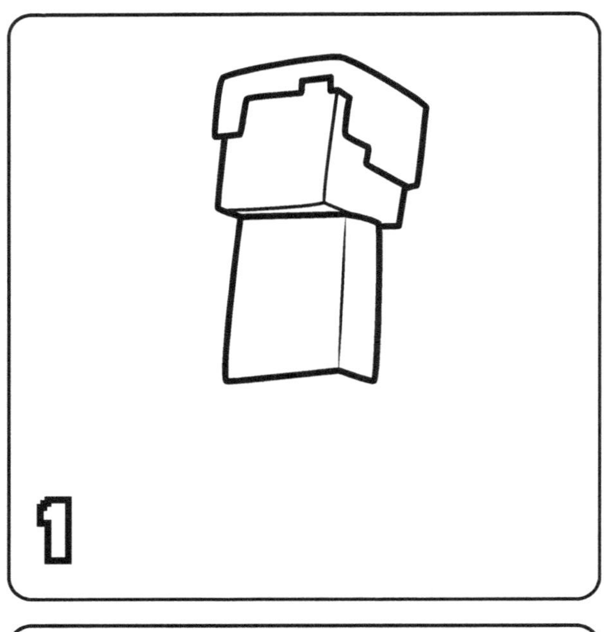

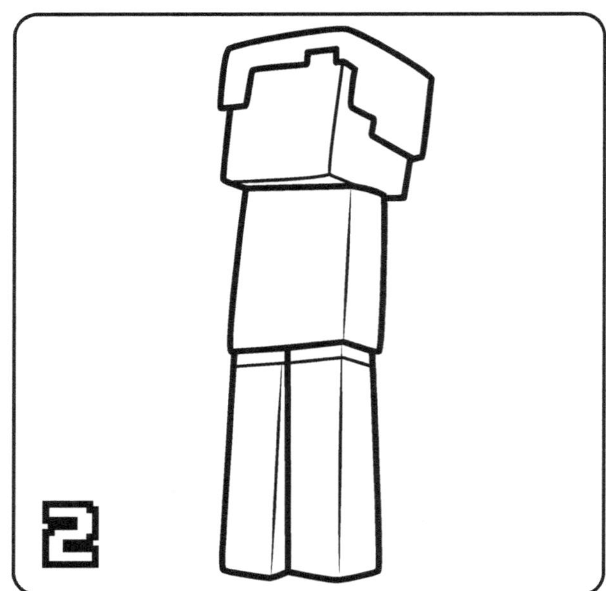

How to draw?
BOB

Now, it's your turn

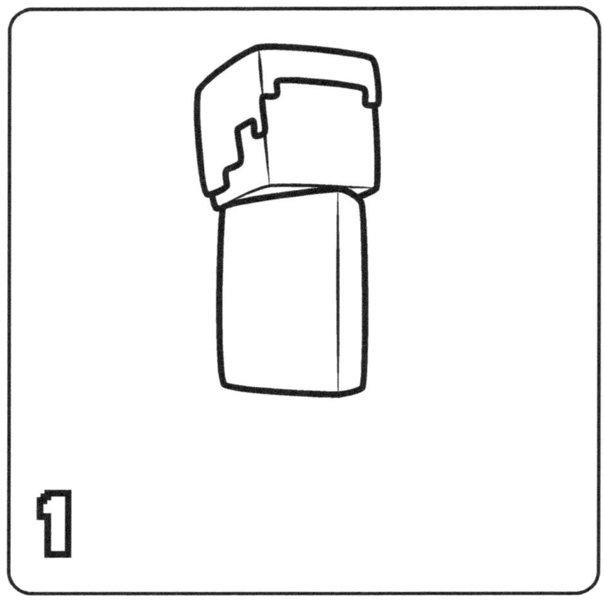

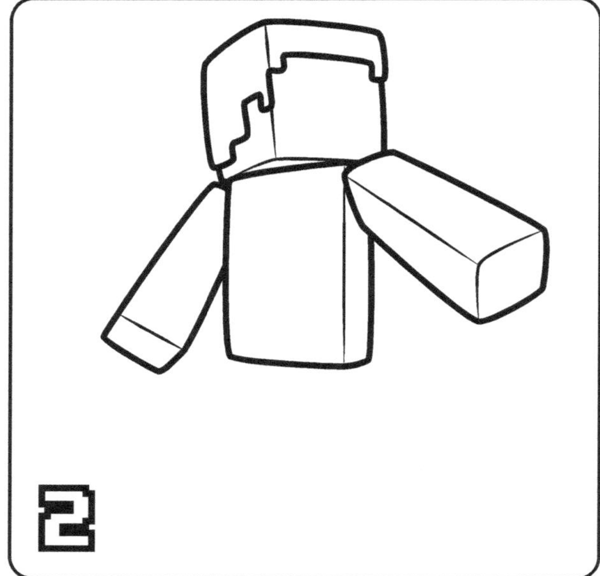

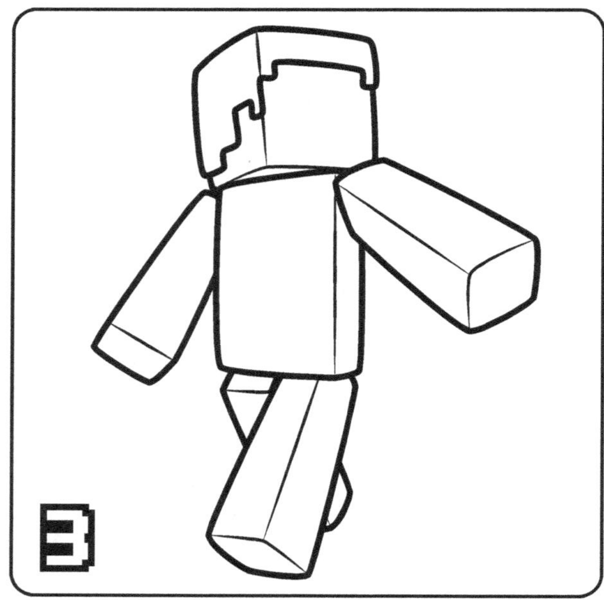

How to draw?
STEVE

Now, it's your turn

How to draw?
MAGMA GOLEM

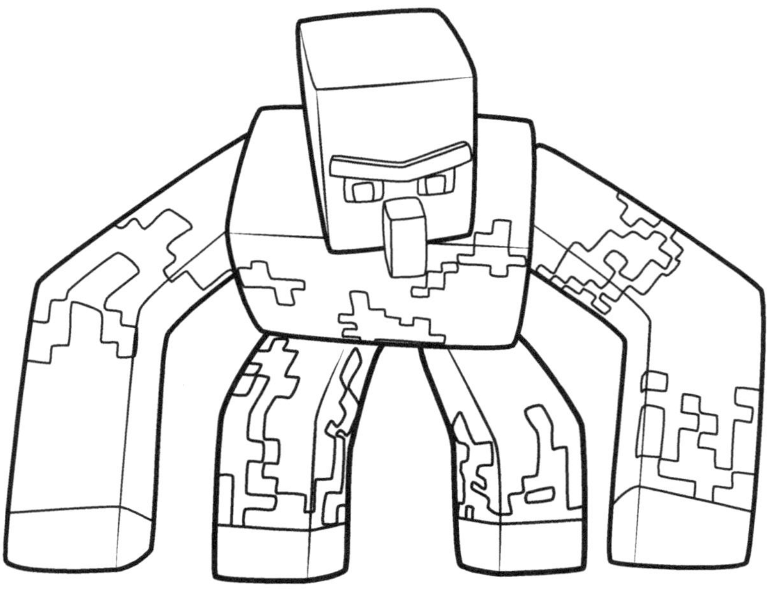

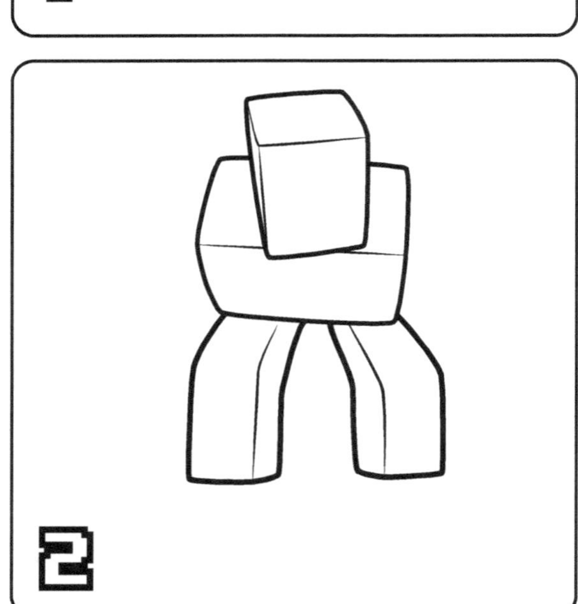

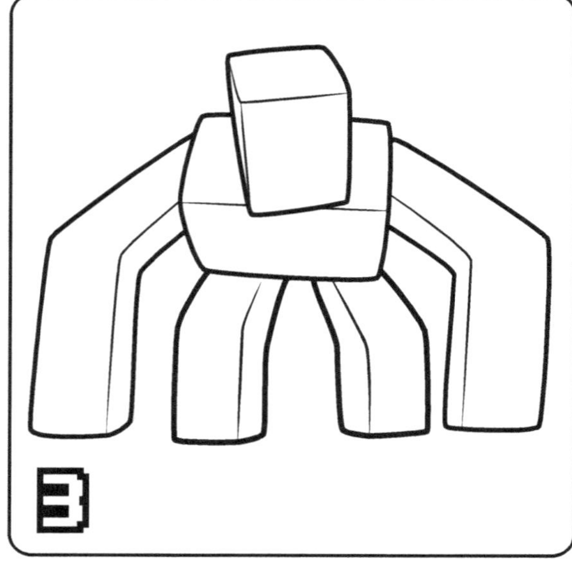

Now, it's your turn

How to draw?

LUKAS

1

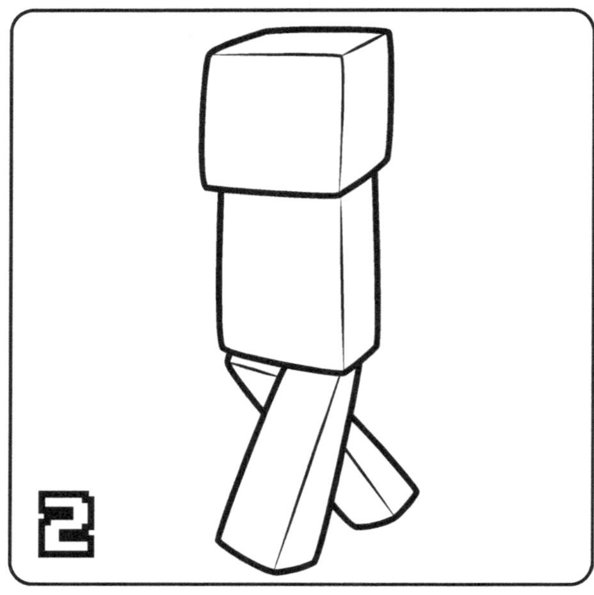

2

3

4

Now, it's your turn

STELLA

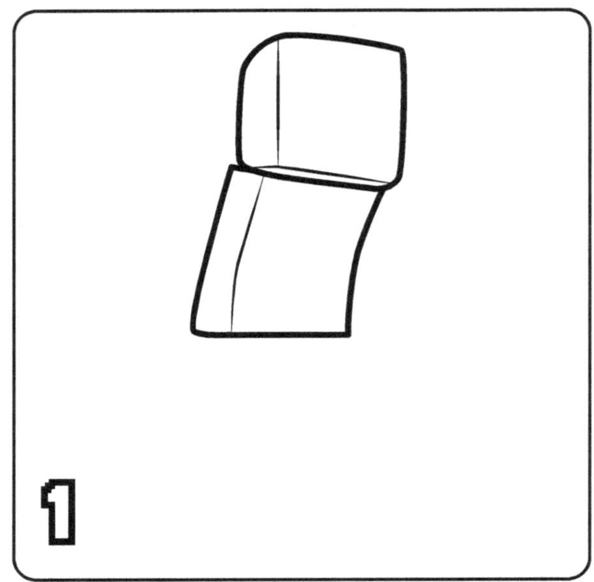

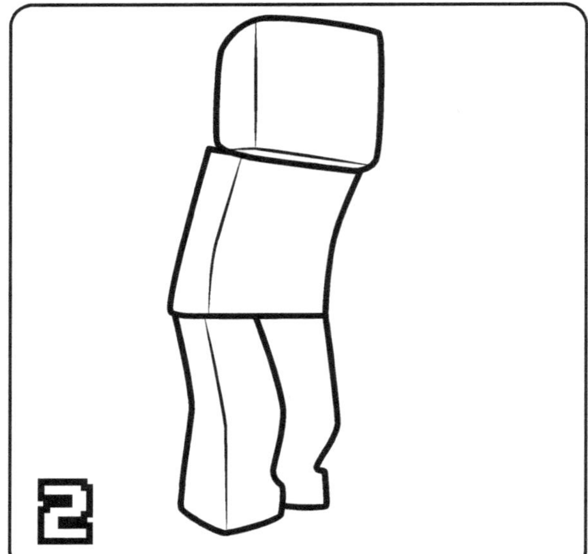

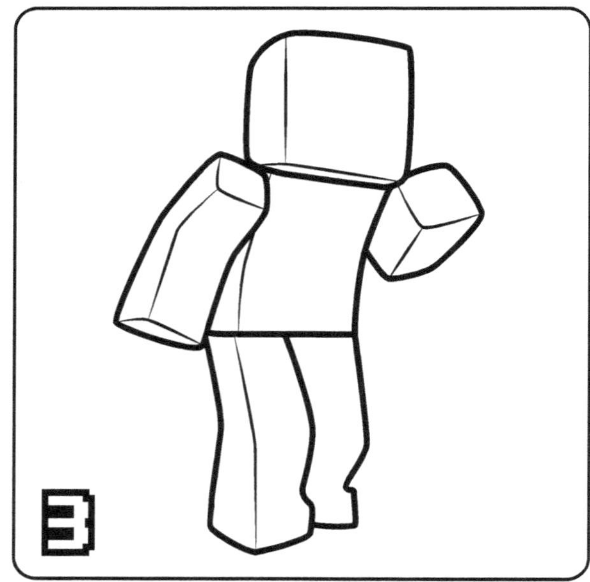

Now, it's your turn

How to draw?
ISA

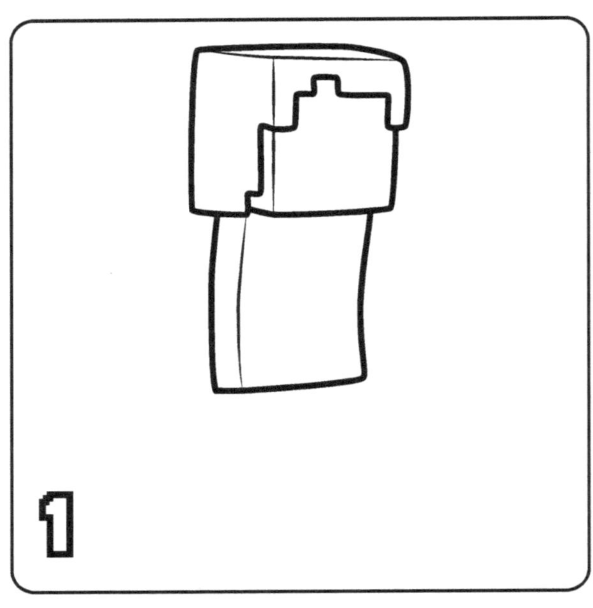

1

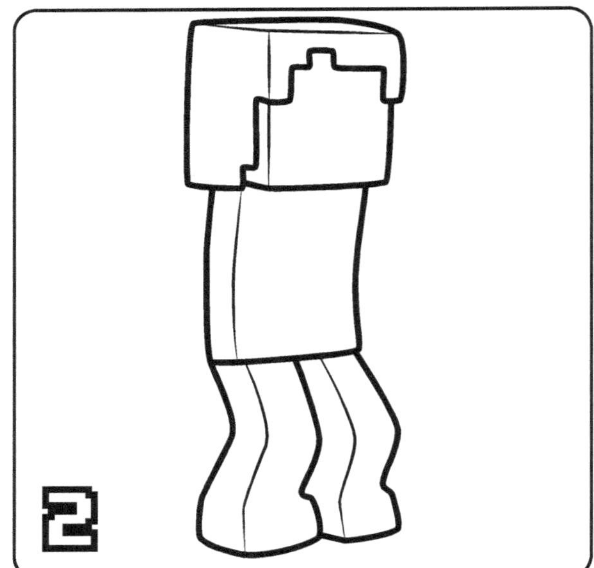

2

3

4

Now, it's your turn

DOWNLOAD 50
FREE COLORING PAGES

Visit our website or message to us!